Gaelic Place Names of the Lothians

GAELIC
PLACE NAMES
OF THE
LOTHIANS

BY

JOHN MILNE, LL.D.

PUBLISHED FOR THE AUTHOR BY
MᶜDOUGALL'S EDUCATIONAL COMPANY, LIMITED.
LONDON : 8 FARRINGDON AVENUE, E.C.
EDINBURGH : 1 AND 2 ST. JAMES SQUARE.

INTRODUCTION.

(*Gaelic words are printed in Italics.*)

THIS little book is intended to give the meaning and the etymology of all the place names of Gaelic origin contained in the six-inch maps of the Ordnance Survey of the Lothians. It was necessary to examine all the names in the maps, because many of them which appear to be English prove to be Gaelic words which had been turned into English words similar in sound but different in meaning, and sometimes they have undergone several transformations.

Arthur's Seat represents *ard-thir suidhe*, place on high ground ; Auld Reekie (High Street, Edinburgh), *alt-ruighe*, high slope ; Guide About, *cuid a' buth*, fold at a shiel. Yellow Man was originally *chuitail*, cattle-fold, which was converted into Whitehill because this resembled *chuitail* in sound. Whitehill was afterwards translated into Gaelic by *ghealach-man* (*ghealach*, white, and *man*, hill). Gh in Gaelic is equivalent to y, and *ghealach* became yallaw in Scotch, which in English became yellow. Among the Gaelic names have been included a few names of English origin.

The examination of the names of places in the Lothians has not brought out the least trace of the Pictish language which some philologists and etymologists imagine was once spoken in Scotland. Cæsar, the first and the best historian of the Roman era in Britain, says that when he was there in 55 and 54 B.C. the inhabitants told him that they were all of one race, and that they were descendants of the first inhabitants of the country. Much has been written on the question whether there was within the Roman period (55 B.C. to 410 A.D.) a people in Scotland called Picts, who differed in race and speech from those whom Cæsar found in Britain. Those who say there was contradict Cæsar, and they ought to prove their statement. The Pictish Question must be settled by evidence written before the departure of the Romans from Britain in 410 A.D. Nothing in later Roman writers, or in Gildas, Bede, Nennius, Adamnan, the Chronicles of the Picts and Scots, or in modern historians, is of importance in this question.

Cæsar says that the Britons stained their bodies blue with woad, but
he does not state whether this was done by an external application or by
inserting the colour into the skin. Probably it was the latter, for the
Roman historian Herodian says that the northern Britons punctured
their bodies with pictured forms of every sort of animals, and wore no
clothes lest they should hide the figures on their bodies. The same
practice had prevailed all over Britain in Cæsar's time, but had been put
down within the Roman Province. Neither Cæsar nor Herodian uses
the term Picts, which is first found in a panegyric delivered by Eumenius
in 287 in praise of Constantius Chlorus on his return from a successful
expedition into Britain He said that till Constantius went against
them the Britons of the south had no more formidable enemy to contend
against than the Picts and Hibernians, but that Constantius easily made
them yield to the Roman arms By Picts he had meant the northern
Britons, who, according to Herodian, punctured coloured figures of
animals into the skin.

In 305 Constantius became emperor and made another expedition into
Britain, taking with him his son Constantine They advanced into
Scotland and established the Roman power ; but Constantius died at
York in 306, and his son, having then become emperor, left Britain to
take up his imperial duties on the Continent. Constantine could hardly
have been a year in Britain, but in 310 Eumenius delivered another
panegyric in which in the emperor's own presence he said that he had
gone to the utmost bound of the island and had undergone hardships
and dangers in the woods and marshes of the Caledonians and other
Picts. He followed Herodian but brought in all the names of places and
peoples in and around Scotland mentioned in antecedent writers,
Ptolemy excepted, in whom he had placed no confidence. The whole
panegyric has been characterised as a string of "outrageous hyperboles."
By Picts he meant all the tattooed Britons north of the English wall, and
he used the term not as a national name but as a descriptive epithet
Following Tacitus he used the name Caledonians to denote the people
living north of the Scotch wall. The phrase "Caledonians and other
Picts" is the base on which the Pictish myth rests. Constantine
adopted Christianity as the religion of the Roman Empire in 330, but
he had done nothing to foster Christianity in Britain, and there is no
allusion to it in the ancient names of places in Scotland.

The Picts are also mentioned by Ammianus Marcellinus, who, though
a Greek, wrote a Latin history of the Roman Empire. He is also the
first to mention the Scots Referring to the period 350 to 360, he states
that incursions of the fierce Scots and Picts wasted the places near the
Roman wall in England. At a later date (368) they extended their
ravages as far south as London, and the Roman Emperor sent Theodosius
to the help of the Britons. With troops from the Continent he advanced

into Britain and near London came upon plundering bands wandering about Some were laden with baggage, others were driving captives and cattle, both no doubt destined to be killed and eaten when the plunderers arrived at their own homes. Where these were we are not told ; but it must have been north of the Roman wall, for Theodosius returned in 369, and having restored the camps and fortifications again extended the boundary of the empire to the Scotch wall and placed watchmen upon it. The district between the English and the Scotch walls was formed into a province and called Valentia in honour of the Emperor Valentinian If the invaders had been transmarine peoples these measures would have done no good to the Romanised Britons in England. Neither Picts nor Scots was a national name, but only a descriptive epithet given by the Britons whom they harassed. Picts comes from a Latin word *pictus*, meaning painted, and Scots might represent one of the Greek words *skotos*, darkness, and *skutos*, hide, and mean either dark complexioned or wearing dressed skins for clothing. Ammianus was a Greek and would have selected a Greek word to furnish an apposite epithet for the invaders.

Claudian, who wrote about 397, mentions the Scots and the Picts, but being a poet and also a panegyrist he sacrificed accuracy in geography to the exigencies of metre The Scots he placed in Ireland and the Picts in Thule. No doubt he had seen captives from Scotland fighting to the death in Roman theatres, and he had been struck by the strange appearance of their tattooed faces, and he speaks of a soldier examining the figures on the face of a dying Pict

In 410 the Romans left Britain, never to return, and then fell on Scotland oblivion as impenetrable as that which shrouded it before Cæsar's advent in 55 B.C. Bede, an ecclesiastical writer who died in 735, is the father of the untruthful statement that in his time four languages were spoken in Britain—those of the Britons, Picts, Scots, and Angles or Saxons. Based upon this statement fictitious chronicles were compiled, giving brief histories of the Picts and the Scots. The history of Scotland cannot be regarded as credible till the Picts and Scots cease to be mentioned in it, because they were held to be different in race from the original Britons In 889 Scotland was called by the native name Alban and its kings were no longer called " Kings of the Picts ' but "Kings of Alban," which title continued to be given to them till the death of Donald (1097), the last king of Alban.

With the accession of Edgar, son of Malcolm Canmore and the English princess Margaret of England, there came a change in the names of the country and its people, and at the same time the language of the country began to undergo a change. In some of Edgar's charters, which are supposed to be the oldest documents written in Scotland, he is called " King of the Scots," this title being reintroduced from the old English Chronicles. The charters are supposed to be genuine, but attributing to Edgar the title "King of the Scots" makes this doubtful.

Malcolm Canmore and his wife were brought up in England, and they could not have been familiar with Gaelic, which was spoken universally in Britain in Cæsar's time but had ceased to be spoken in England, though it was still the language of Scotland. In their family and at their court English had begun to displace Gaelic, and this change had been complete in the reign of Edgar, for one of his charters is attested by the signatures of Saxons. He had made Edinburgh his residence and the use of English had soon become general in the Lothians. Gaelic had rapidly given way before English till the death of Alexander III in 1286. Probably the process had slackened during the interregnum and the Bruce period, but it had been again accelerated after 1371, when the Stuart period began. After the return of James I. from captivity in England the decay of Gaelic had been rapid. Gaelic is a very old language, probably the oldest language spoken at the present day. When Cæsar came to Britain in 55 B.C. he found that it was spoken all over the island called Britannia, and we know that the language of Ireland was anciently identical with that of Scotland. But there is good reason to believe that Gaelic was spoken in Britain at least 2000 years B.C. The oldest work constructed by man to be seen in Britain is Stonehenge, where there are four concentric circles of stones on a hill-side, eight miles from Salisbury. One of the stones stands more than twenty feet out of the ground, and though it had been dressed into a rectangular form with enormous expenditure of labour, yet there is no mark of a metal tool upon it. Archæologists say that the use of bronze was not known in Britain till about 2000 B.C. and that the circles must have been erected before that date. The oldest form of the name is Stanenges, which is a corruption of the Gaelic words *S[i]*[he]*an* [*Fh*]*augan*, hill of circles, in which the letters within brackets had become silent and had been lost. Final an had normally become es. The circles at Stonehenge guard a grave in the centre, and there are many circles of tall stone pillars round graves in Scotland. Most of these show no marks of metal tools, but some, probably more recent, have cups upon them which had been cut out with metal chisels. These Scotch circles may be as old as those of Stonehenge, and they are without doubt the work of our remote Gaelic-speaking ancestors. The etymologist soon discovers that the Gaelic of the place names is different from that now in use. Modern Gaelic is cumbered with expedients for indicating gender, number, and case, but old Gaelic has few of these grammatical contrivances, and it is as a rule best to ignore them in etymology.

Every person whose mother-tongue is Gaelic can make out the meaning of some names of places and persons, and a person provided with a Gaelic dictionary can make out a few more; but he soon finds that a dictionary is of little use to him unless he knows a good deal of Gaelic grammar. Hence a few notes are subjoined to help the etymologist over some of the stiles that bar his progress.

There are in Gaelic eighteen letters, a, b, c, d, e, f, g, i, l, m, n, o, p, r, s, t, u, to which may be added h. Nine of these, b, c, d, f, g, m, p, s, t are liable to have their sound changed, or they may become silent and then be omitted. Of these, c, f, s, t, may be changed to h, and h is put after them to show when this takes place. In Irish the change is indicated by a round dot above the letter. In fh both f and h may become silent and may be lost. Bh is sounded as u, v, w, or ou, and mh has the same sounds but they are slightly nasal, and an after mh may become ng. Dh and gh are both sounded as y, and ph is sounded as f.

One reason for making these changes is to indicate that there is some connection between two words when one of them begins with the sound of h, v, or y ; and another is to facilitate pronunciation. It is easier to sound h than c, f, s, or t ; v than b or m ; y than d or g, and p than f. In Gaelic d had often the sound of dg or dj ; hence *dearg* is made jarg, and *aod* is made edge. Adding h to a letter is called aspirating it, though this term is not in all cases appropriate. Aspirated letters are soft and are liable to be left out, and the etymologist must be prepared for finding any aspirated letter substituted for any other aspirated letter. Ch often becomes wh, or ph which is the same as f. Bh and mh are often interchanged, and dh and gh sometimes take the place of one another.

Final an in Gaelic causes "much trouble to the inexperienced etymologist. It may be three things. It may be a radical part of a word, a diminutive termination, or a plural termination. In all three cases, especially in the first, it may remain unchanged in passing into Scotch. In the second, an may become na by transposing a and n, and na may become nie, ney, ny, or less frequently nay. Sometimes n in an is dropped, and the obscure final a may become in Scotch ie, y, or less frequently o or och. In the third case an usually becomes es or s, but sometimes ee or se. Mistakes are of frequent occurrence. Radical an may be found changed to ie and e, as if it were a diminutive termination, or to s as if it were a plural termination. Diminutive an is sometimes though rarely changed to s. This is common in English names of Gaelic origin. Sometimes an has been left unchanged, but ie has been added to an instead of being substituted for it. The plural termination an is sometimes left unchanged, but s had been added to it instead of being substituted for it.

The letter s is often intruded into the middle of a word to convert the first part into an English possessive qualifying the second. This is common when the first part ends in n.

The letter m was often followed by b when a Gaelic word passed into

Scotch. *Cam*, crooked, became camb. Final n occasionally takes on euphonic c or k as in sink for *sithean*—th and its vowels being lost. D is frequently added for euphony to n as in names containing land, where lan represents *lamhan* (mh silent), hill. St for Saint as the first part of a place name frequently represents *sithean*, hill—th with its vowels becoming silent and euphonic t being added to n. In the Aberdeenshire name St Cloud St is Saint for *sithean*, hill, to which had afterwards been added as an explanation *cnoc*, corrupted into cloud as in cloudberry, mountain berry. In the names Great Saint Bernard and Little Saint Bernard the last two words represent *sithean*, hill; *bearn*, pass or gap; and *ard*, hill.

No Gaelic word begins with a radical h, but it was often prefixed to words beginning with a vowel when they passed into Scotch.

J.M.

PLACE NAMES

OF

MIDLOTHIAN

GAELIC
PLACE NAMES
OF
MIDLOTHIAN

BY

JOHN MILNE, LL.D.

PUBLISHED FOR THE AUTHOR BY
M⸰DOUGALL'S EDUCATIONAL COMPANY, LIMITED.
LONDON :   8 FARRINGDON AVENUE, E.C.
EDINBURGH : 1 AND 2 ST. JAMES SQUARE.

PLACE NAMES OF
MIDLOTHIAN

ADAM BRAE. Brae. *Aodann*, brae. The second part is a translation of the first

ADAMS RIG. Brae. *Aodann*, brae Ann was improperly made s instead of ie, and s instead of being substituted for ann was added to it.

ADAMSROW. Both parts of the name mean brae. *Aodann*, brae, *ruigh*, slope of a hill

ADDIEWELL BRAE. Town on a brae. *Baile*, town, *aodann*, brae. To avoid a hiatus *baile* had been put last and made *bhaile*, pronounced waile and now made well. Ann became ie.

ADDISTON. Town on a brae. *Aodann*, brae. Ann had normally become ie, and s had been added to ie to obtain an English possessive.

ADIE'S SIKE Burn from a brae. *Aodann*, brae. Ann had been made both ie and s.

AIKENDEAN. Den of the fold. *Aigheann*, fold.

AIMVILLE BURN. Burn. *Amhainn*, stream. Mh is sounded v, and m ought to have been dropped when v was introduced. Final nn often becomes ll, as in cill for *cinn*. *Amhainn* had become avainn and subsequently availl, and aimville.

AIRFIELD Field on a shieling. *Airidh*, shieling.

AIVEN SYKE. Small stream forming the head of a burn *Abhainn*, river, burn.

ALDERSTONE Stone at a burn on a shieling. *Allt*, burn *airidh*, shieling Dh, being silent, had been lost

ALLAN'S HAUGH Haugh at a small burn *Allan*, diminutive of *all*, stream. S had been inserted to make *allan* possessive.

ALLERMUIR. Muir of the hill of the shieling. *Aill*, hill *airidh*, shieling.

ALMOND. Burn from a hill *All*, burn; *monadh*, hill

ALNWICK Nook of the burn. *Uig*, nook; *allan*, small stream.

AMAZONDEAN This name means den of a town in a beautiful place. A is an addition made to obtain an English word; maz represents *maise*, beauty; on is for town, and dean is for the Gaelic word *dein*, den.

ANKRIELAW, for *An Creag Lamh* The hill. *An*, the, *creach*, hill; *lamh*, hill.

ANNETSCROSS. Crossing at the junction of two streams. *Crois*, crossing; *aonadh*, junction.

ANN'S MILL. Mill at a fold. *Innis*, enclosed place.

ARMET WATER. Burn draining good land. *Ar*, land, *meith*, good.

ARNISTON. Town of watching cattle at night *Airnean* (Irish), watching. Ean had been made i as a diminutive and s as a plural termination.

ARNOTT BOO, for *Buth Airne Noadh*. House where a watch was kept. *Buth* (th silent), hut; *airne*, watch; *noadh*, watching. The last part explains the second.

ARTHUR'S SEAT, for *Ard-thir Suidhe*. Place on high ground. *Ard* height; *thir*, *tir* aspirated, land; *suidhe*, place, situation. *Suidhe* had once been first, but it had been translated and put last.

ASHBROOK. Both parts mean burn. *Eas* (pron. ash), burn.

ASHLEY. Grassy place at a burn. *Eas* burn; ley (Scotch), grassy place.

AUCHENCORTH. Place of the fold. *Achadh*, place; *an*, of the, *corth*, fold, stone circle.

AUCHENDINNY. Place at a little hill. *Achadh*, place; *an*, of the; *dunan*, little hill

AUCHENHARROW. Place of the shieling. *Achadh*, place; *an*, of the; *airidh*, shieling.

AUCHINOON. Place for lambs. *Achadh*, place; *an*, of the; *uan*, lamb

BAAD PARK. Enclosed wood. *Bad*, bush, wood; *pairc*, park.

BAADS. Small wood. *Badan*, small bushy place. *An* had improperly been made s instead of ie.

BABERTON. Town at a fold on a shieling. *Babhunn*, milking fold; *airidh*, shieling. Unn changed to ie had been lost before *airidh*.

BACK DRUM. North side of a ridge. *Druim*, long ridge. Back might be *bac*, moss.

BACK OF MOSS MOSS. *Bac*, moss. The second part is a translation of the first.

BACKDALE. If this name is Gaelic it represents *Dail Bac*. Field of the moss *Dail*, field; *bac*, peat-moss If it is English it means dell on the north side of a hill. Back, north-lying; dale, valley, dell.

BACKDEAN. Valley on the north side of a hill. *Dein*, dean, den, gorge eroded by ice or running water.

BACKSIDE. If this name is English it means north side of a hill. If it is Gaelic it means place in a moss. *Suidhe*, place, site; *bac*, moss.

BAILEYFIELD, for *Achadh Baile*. Field near a town. *Achadh*, field; *baile*, town

BALERNO. Town where a watch was kept. *Baile*, town; *airne*, watching cattle against thieves.

BALLENY. Place full of little knolls. *Bailleanach*, abounding in knolls.

BALLGREEN. Sunny town. *Baile*, town; *grianach*, sunny, warm.

BANGHOLM. Fold Originally *Chuitail*, *cuitail* aspirated, fold, corrupted into whitehill, which was again turned into Gaelic by *bantholm*, white hill (*ban*, white , *tholm*, *tolm* aspirated, hill) *Tolm* was aspirated because it followed its adjective Euphonic g had been added to *ban*, and t in *tholm* had been lost.

BANK HEAD, BANKHEAD If English this name means head of a high level terrace. If Gaelic it represents *Chuit Chuid*, both of which mean fold *Chuit* had been corrupted into white, which had subsequently been turned into Gaelic by *ban*, white, with k added for euphony. To explain bank *chuid*, *cuid* aspirated, fold, had been added to it, but c being silent in ch it had been lost, leaving huid, which had been made head in the belief that it was an English word

BANKTON. Town on the bank of a burn.

BARBACHLAW. Point of the big hill. *Barr*, point , *bagach*, bulky , *lamh*, hill G with its vowel had been dropped

BARLEY KNOWE Point on the side of a knoll *Barr*, point; *leth* (th silent), side.

BARLEYDEAN Point on the side of a den. *Barr*, point; *leth* (th silent), *dein*, dean, den

BARNTON. Town in a hollow. *Bearn*, gap in a ridge, long trench–like hollow in a level plain.

BARON'S CLEUGH Gap between two steep banks *Bearnas*, gap.

BARTHOLOMEW'S FIRLOT, for *Feur-lot Barr Tholm Chuith*. Hay-loft for a fold on the point of a small round hill *Feur-lot*, hay loft , *barr*, point , *tholm*, *tolm* aspirated, round hillock; *chuith*, *cuith* aspirated, fold *Chuith* lost ch and th, and ui is now pronounced ew. S was added to turn Bartholomew into the possessive

BAVELAND, for *Lamh Babhunn* Hill of the fold. *Lamh*, hill , *babhunn*, fold. Unn had become ie, which had been lost

BAWDY MOSS Bushy moss *Badach*, bushy

BEATMAN'S ACRE, for *Ard-thir Man Beathach*. High cultivated land on a hill where birches grow. *Ard*, high , *thir*, *tir* aspirated, land , *man*, hill , *beathach*, abounding in birches. Acre for *ard-thir* is found in the name Acrestripe

BEESLACK Gorge of birches *Beith*, birch; *slochd*, gorge, howe.

BEGGAR'S BUSH. Bushy place on a little shieling Beggars, for *Beag Airidh*, small shieling *Beag*, small , *airidh*, shieling.

BELL LAW, BELLFIELD, BELL'S HILL, BELL'S LAW, BELL'S MAINS, BELLOWS BRAE, BELLYFORD, BELSTANE. The first part of the names is *Buaile*, fold Law is *lamh*, hill , mains is *man*, hill, with s added because ain was erroneously regarded as a plural termination ; and brae is *braigh*, hill

BENRY. Slope of a hill. *Ruigh*, slope; *beinn*, hill.

BENT'S HILL. Little hill. *Beanntan*, diminutive of *beann*, hill. An had improperly been made s.

BENTIEHEAD, for *Beanntan Chuid*. Little hill on which there was a fold. *Beanntan*, diminutive of *beann*, hill; *chuid, cuid* aspirated, fold. C silent had been lost.

BERRY KNOWE. Pointed hill. *Biorach*, pointed.

BERRYHILL. Watery hill. *Biorach*, watery.

BINKS. Fold. Originally *Chuitail, cuitail* aspirated, fold, corrupted into whitehill, which was again turned into Gaelic by *beinncan*, white hill. An in *can* is not a plural termination but it was made s. Beinncs is now binks.

BIRK BURN. Burn bordered by birch-trees.

BIRNIEHILL, BIRNY KNOWE, BIRNY ROCKS   The first part is *Bearna*, gap into hill, or long hollow in level ground.

BLACK MOUNT, BLACK RIG, BLACK TOE, BLACKBRAE, BLACK-COT, BLACKDUB, BLACKHALL, BLACKHILL, BLACKHOPE, BLACKLAW, BLACKRAW, BLACKSIDE RIG. In most of these names Black had originally been *dubh*, black; but in some it may be a corruption of *bleoghann*, milking-place, in which ann became ie, afterwards lost. Mount is *monadh*, hill; rig is *ruigh*, slope; toe is a point where two burns meet; brae is *braigh*, hill; cot is *cuit*, fold; dub is *dubh*, black, hall is *choill, coill* aspirated, hill, with c silent lost; hope is *chop, cop* aspirated, hill, with c silent lost; law is *lamh*, hill, raw is *rath*, fold; side is *suidhe*, seat, place.

BLAW WEARY, for *Blath Chuith Airidh*. Pleasant fold on a shieling. *Blath*, warm, pleasant; *chuith, cuith* aspirated, fold; *airidh*, shieling. The aspirated letters were lost, being silent. Ui is sounded as we.

BLINKBONNY. Milking-place in a hollow. *Bleoghann* (gh silent), milking; *bonnan*, diminutive of *bonn*, bottom, hollow.

BOGHALL. Farm house at a bog. Hall represents the kitchen, the public room in a farm-house.

BOLL OF BEAR, for *Poll Bior*. Pool of water. *Poll*, pool; *bior*, water.

BONALLY. Bottom of a hill; *Bonn*, bottom; *aill*, hill. The sound of y is heard after *aill* when forcibly pronounced.

BONAR'S WELL. Well at a summer shiel. *Bothan* (th silent), hut; *airidh*, shiel. S made Bonar possessive.

BONNINGTON. Farm town in a small howe. *Bonnan*, diminutive of *bonn*, bottom, howe.

BONNYFIELD, BONNYRIG. Place in a hollow, and Slope at a hollow. *Bonnan*, little hollow; *ruigh*, slope.

BORE STANE. Big Stone. *Borr*, big.

BORTHWICK, for *Uig Chorth*. Nook of the fold. *Uig*, nook; *chorth, corth* aspirated, fold. *Chorth* had subsequently been made bhorth and borth.

Bow. Curve in a hillside. *Bogha*, bend.

Bow BRIDGE. Bridge with an arch. *Bogha*, curve.

Bow Hill, perhaps Cow-hill. *Bo*, cow.

Bowbeat Hill. Hill with a curve in which birch-trees grow. *Bogha*, bend ; *beath*, birch

Bower, for *Bo-airidh*. Summer pasture for cows. *Bo*, cow ; *airidh* (idh silent), shieling.

Bowland. Cow-hill *Bo*, cow ; *lamhan*, hill, with euphonic d added.

Bowlee. Grass-land where cows fed *Bo*, cow ; ley (Scotch), grassy place.

Bowman's Gill. Cow-hill glen *Bo*, cow , *man*, hill ; *gill*, small ravine. *Gill* is said to be Norse, but it seems to have been adopted into Gaelic. *Gill* is a common word in the northwest of England.

Bowshank, for *Bo-sithean* Cow-hill. *Bo*, cow ; *sithean* (th silent), hill Euphonic k had been added to n

Bradlaw. Hill *Braghad* (gh silent), hill , *lamh*, hill.

Brae End, for *Braighean* Little hill. *Braighean*, diminutive of *braigh*, hill. Euphonic d had been added to n.

Braid Burn, Braid Hill, Braid Law, Braidwood. The first part is *braid* (Irish), hill Law is *lamh*, hill.

Breich Bridge, Breich Water. Breich is *bruch*, hill.

Brewer's Bush. Bushy place on a shieling hill. *Bruch*, hill ; *airidh*, shieling.

Brierybaulk Uncultivated ridge growing briers Brier, wild rose, from *preas*, bush ; balk, strip of land between two cultivated ridges.

Brieston. Town on a small hill. *Braighean*, diminutive of *braigh*, hill. Gh is equal to y, and ean had been made s though it is a diminutive termination.

Brigs, for *Bruchan* Small hill *Bruchan*, diminutive of *bruch*, hill. An ought to have become ie

Brockhouse. Hill of the fold *Bruch*, hill ; *chuith*, *cuith* aspirated, fold C in ch is silent and had been lost, and th had become sh, afterwards losing the aspirate. It is unlikely that house is the English word.

Brookbank. Bank of a hill. *Bruch*, hill

Broomhill. Hill growing broom. Some proprietors required tenants to sow broom to be thatch for houses.

Brosie Mains, perhaps for *Bruthach Main*. Ascent of a hill. *Bruthach*. ascent ; *main*, genitive of *man*, hill. Th and sh have the same sound, and hence t and s are sometimes used the one for the other. Final am had been thought to be a plural termination, hence s had been added to n.

Brotchrig, for *Ruigh Bruch* Slope of the hill. *Ruigh*, slope ; *bruch*, hill. *Bruch* had been strengthened by inserting t.

Brothershiels. Huts on the hill of the shieling. *Sealan*, huts for people in charge of cattle on a shieling , *bruch*, hill ; *airidh*, shieling, summer pasture

Brotherstone. Stone on the hill of the shieling. *Bruch*, hill , *airidh*, shieling Stone might be ton, town, with s prefixed.

BROUGHTON. Hill town. *Bruch*, hill.

BROWN MOOR BURN. Moor of the burn. Brown, for *braon*, hill burn.

BRUCEFIELD. Hill field. *Bruch*, hill.

BRUCEHILL. Hill. The second part is a translation of the first. *Bruch*, hill.

BRUNSTANE, for *Clach Braon*. Stone at a burn. *Clach*, stone; *braon* burn.

BRUNSTON Burn town. *Braon*, hill burn. S represents aon of *braon*, regarded as a plural termination.

BRUNTSFIELD. Field at a burn. *Braon*, hill burn. T is euphonic, and s represents aon regarded as a plural termination. In Burntisland, which represents *braon lamhan*, burn of the hill, aon has been made is, which has changed land, meaning hill, into island.

BRYANS. Little hill. *Braighean*, diminutive of *braigh*, hill. An became s instead of ie.

BUCKSTONE SNAB. Meaning uncertain. Perhaps big stone on a blunt point. *Buchd*, bigness, big; snab (Scotch), blunt point.

BUGHELIN. Cow-stalls. *Buaighealean*, plural of *buaigheal*, cow-stall.

BUISELAW, for *Buidhe Lamh*. Yellow hill. *Buidhe*, yellow, growing broom; *lamh* (mh silent), hill. S is an insertion made to obtain an English possessive.

BURDIEHOUSE. House on a small flat place. *Bordan*, little level place. An became ie.

BURGESS CAIRN. Cairn at a hill-burn. *Carn*, cairn; *bruch*, hill; *eas* (pronounced ess), burn, waterfall.

BURGHLEE. Grassy place on a hill. *Bruch*, hill; ley (Scotch), level grass-land.

BURNDALE. Burnfield. *Dail*, field.

BURNGRANGE, for Burngrains. Space between two arms of a burn. Grain, same as groin.

BURNHALL. Farm-house at a burn. Hall means the farm-kitchen, the public place in the house.

BURNHEAD, for *Braon Chuid*. Burn of the fold. *Braon*, burn; *chuid*, *cuid* aspirated, fold. C silent had been lost, and huid had become head. This place is not at the head of a burn.

BURNWYND, for *Braon Bheinn*. Burn of the hill. *Braon*, burn; *bheinn*, *beinn* aspirated, hill. Bh is equivalent to w.

BUSHDYKE. Black clump of trees. Bush, group of trees; *dubh*, black.

BUTELAND. House on a hill. *Buth*, hut, house; *lamhan*, hill. Mh in *lamhan* is silent, and euphonic d had been added to n.

BUTTERFIELD, BUTTERHALL. Butter is for *Buth Airidh*. Hut on a shieling. *Buth*, hut, shiel; *airidh*, shieling. Hall is *choill*, *coill* aspirated, hill, c silent being lost.

BYE LAW. Birch Hill. *Beith* (th silent), birch; *lamh*, hill.

BYRES LOAN. Grass-land at cow-byres 'on a shieling. Loan, grassy place; *buth*, (th silent), hut for cows; *airidh* (idh silent), shieling. Bu-air became byre.

BYERSIDE HILL. Watery hillside. *Bior*, water, burn.

CADAMSCLEUGH. The space between the steep sides of a ravine *Cadam*, division.

CADGER'S HOME, for *Cadha Thom*. Hill road. *Cadha*, road, track; *thom*, *tom* aspirated, hill. T is silent.

CAERKETTON CRAIGS, for *Creagan Cathair Cuitan*. Little hill which was the seat of a fold. *Creagan*, diminutive of *creag*, hill, *cathair* (th silent), *seat*; *cuitan*, diminutive of *cuit*, fold.

CAIRNS. Small hill. *Carnan*, diminutive of *carn*, hill. *Carnan* is also the plural of *carn*, and it might mean hills.

CAIRNSMUIR. Little hill on a muir. *Carnan*, little hill. An was improperly made s instead of ie

CAIRNTOWS. Hill in a little hollow *Carn*, hill, cairn; *tollan*, diminutive of *toll*, howe. Oll becomes ou or ow.

CAIYSIDE. Site of a fold. *Suidhe*, site, *cuidh* (dh equal to y), fold. A stone with incised cups marks a prehistoric grave.

CAKEMUIR. Muir of the burn. *Caoch*, burn howe.

CALDCOT, for *Cul Cuit*. Back fold *Cul*, back; *cuit*, fold. D is a euphonic insertion.

CALDER, for *Callaidh Dobhar*. Swift water. *Callaidh*, swift, *dobhar*, (bh silent), water, burn

CALFHOPE. Hollow of the hill. *Cabh*, hollow, *chop*, *cop* aspirated, hill. C in ch being silent, had been lost.

CALTON Little hill *Coilltean*, diminutive of *coill*, hill.

CAMERON, for *Cam-sron*. Crooked nose. The nose is a narrow bit of land within a bend of Braid Burn.

CAMILTY. Many roads *Cath* (th silent), road, *milteach*. very many. The roads were concentric ditches surrounding an ancient fold.

CAMP, CAMP HILL. The camps were cattle-folds

CAMP BRIDGE. A ridge at a crook in a burn. *Cam*, crooked.

CAMPEND, for *Caman*. Small curve. *Camun*, diminutive of *cam*, crooked, bent. P and d are euphonic additions to m and n

CAMSTONE QUARRY. Camstone is a white decayed felspathic or else calcareous rock. formerly sold in small blocks for rubbing door-steps on Saturday that they might be white on Sunday. *Can*, white.

CANNIEHOLE, for *Ceann na Choille*. Head of the hill *Ceann*, head; *na*, of the, *choille*, *coille*, hill. C silent had been lost

CANNY KNOWES Knolls where mountain cotton (eriophorum) grows. *Canach*, cotton grass, cats-tail

CANTYHALL Little head on the hill. *Ceanntan*, diminutive of *ceann*, head, *choill*, *coill* aspirated, hill. An normally became y.

CAP LAW, CAPELAW. Hill. *Cap*, summit, hill; *lamh*, hill

CAPIELAW. Hill. *Ceapan*, diminutive of *ceap*, hill, *lamh*, hill.

CARBERRY HILL. The three parts all mean hill. *Cathair* (th silent), hill; *bruch*, hill.

CARBERRY TROWS. The arable farm at Carberry. *Treobhachas*, cultivated land. Bh is equal to w, and ch with its vowels had been lost.

CARBOTHIE. Hill of the little house. *Cathair* (th silent), hill; *bothan*, small hut. An became ie.

CARCANT NICK, for *Na Eag Cathair Canta*. The gap of a hill where there was a pool. *Na*, the, *eag*, nick, gap; *cathair* (th silent), hill; *canta*, lake, pool.

CARLEHALL. Hill. *Cathair* (th silent), hill; *lamh* (mh silent), hill; *choill, coill* aspirated, hill. C in ch is silent.

CARLOPS, for *Luban Cathair*. Little bend in a hill. *Luban*, diminutive of *lub*, bend; *cathair* (th silent), hill. An was wrongly made s instead of ie.

CARNETHY. Hill of the little burn. *Carn*, hill; *nethan*, little burn. An normally became y.

CARRINGTON. Town at a little fold. *Cathairean*, diminutive of *cathair*, fold, hill Th is silent and had been lost. Bell Law at Carrington shows that there was a fold on a small hill there. See Bell Law.

CARSEWELL. Town on a hill. *Bhaile, baile* aspirated, town; *cathair* (th silent), hill. *Baile* had originally been first, but it had been put last and aspirated and made well, bh being equal to w. S made car possessive.

CARSINKER LAW, for *Lamh Cathair Sithean Airidh*. Hill of the shieling. *Lamh*, hill; *cathair*, hill; *sithean*, hill; *airidh*, shieling. All the aspirated letters had been lost, and k had been added to n for euphony.

CASTLE GREY. Castle or fort on a hill. *Creag*, hill. The supposed fort is an ancient cattle-fold.

CASTLE o' CLOUTS. Mansion built by a clothier.

CASTLELAW. Castle hill. *Lamh*, hill.

CAT HAUGH. Haugh of the path. *Cat*, path, drove road

CAT NICK ROAD. Notch in which there was a path. *Cat*, road; nick (Scotch), notch.

CAT STANE. Stone showing a right of way. *Cat*, footpath, drove road

CATCUNE. Steep road. *Cat*, road; *cuinge*, steepness, difficulty.

CATHA RIG. Road on the slope of a hill. *Catha*, drove road, *ruigh*, side of a hill.

CATHIE. Place near a road. *Catha*, road, ravine.

CATPAIR, for *Cath Fair*. Road over a hill. *Cath*, drove road; *fair*, hill. F is equal to ph, and when *cath* lost the aspirate and became *cat* ph had also lost the aspirate and had become p.

CATWELL, for *Bhaile Cat*. Town on a road. *Bhaile, baile* aspirated, town; *cat*, road. Bh is equal to w, and *bhaile* had become well. Well might be an English word.

CAUL Weir. *Caol*, narrow. A fishing weir narrows a river. Euphonic d is sometimes added to l.

CAULD STANE SLAP. Slap with a stone in it on the north side of a hill. *Cul*, back, north.

CAULDCOTS, for *Cuil Cuitan*. Nook of the little fold *Cuil*, nook, *cuitan*, diminutive of *cuit*, fold. An had by mistake been regarded as a plural termination and had been changed to s instead of ie.

CAULDHALL. Nook in a hill. *Cuil*, nook; *choill, coill* aspirated, hill C in ch is silent.

CAUSEWAYEND, CAUSEWAYSIDE. Causeway represents Calceata Via (Latin), shod way. Calceata, protected by stones and gravel; via, way.

CHALKIESIDE. Place on a hill where there was a fold. *Suidhe*, place; *choill, coill* aspirated, hill; *cuith* (th silent), fold.

CHANGE HOUSE House at a fank or fold where sheep and cattle on a journey could be kept at night *Fang*, fank, fold. F or ph, became ch, g hard became soft, and thus *fang* became change. Change house came to mean an inn because there were fanks at inns on drove roads There was a change house at Wrights Houses. Some inns with fanks were called chance inns.

CHARLIE'S WELL, for *Tobar Sear Laos* Well at the black fold. *Tobar*, well, *sear*, dark, black; *laos*, fold. Se is pronounced she.

CHASELY BURN. Burn of the rapid ford. *Cas-lighe*, rapid ford.

CHESTERHILL, CHESTERS. There were anciently cattlefolds at these places, which were afterwards supposed to have been Roman camps. Edgehead near Chesterhill means fold, and there is a trace of a fold at Chesters. Castra (Latin), camp.

CHIRMAT. Big crest of a ridge. *Chir, cir* aspirated, crest; *mata* (Irish), great.

CLAUGHRIE BURN. Burn formerly crossed by a row of stepping stones. *Clacharan*, stepping stones.

CLAYBARNS Offices on a farm, built of clay.

CLAYLANDS. Probably this name means stony hill. *Clachach* (chach lost), stony; *lamhan* (mh silent), hill, with d added for euphony, and s added because *lamhan* ended in an, wrongly supposed to be a plural termination

CLEARBURN. Burn whose water is transparent. As a Gaelic prefix *clar* means in front of, before.

CLEAVE Wattled fold. *Cleath*, wattled fold. Th had become bh, equal to v.

CLEIKIMINN Meaning uncertain, perhaps inn of assemblies. The spelling indicates a confusion between *clich*, to assemble, and *clichd*, iron hook, cleik (Scotch).

CLERKINGTON, for *Baile Clar Cinn*. Town at a broad faced place. *Baile*, town; *clar*, broad; *cinn*, for *ceann*, head.

CLERMISTON. Beautiful town sloping to the south. *Clair*, front, south, *maise*, beautiful. Sometimes the east was regarded as the front side

CLINTY CLEUGH. Steep bank of the little valley. *Cluaintean,* little valley. Ean had normally become y.

CLOVENFORD. Ford at stepping-stones. *Clocharan,* stepping-stones. Ch had become bh, equal to v, and r had been lost.

CLOVERFOOT, for *Clochar Chuit.* Stony fold. *Clochar,* stony; *chuit, cuit* aspirated, fold. Ch of *clochar* had become bh, equal to v, and ch in *chuit* had become ph, equal to f.

CLUBBIE DEAN, for *Clumhach Dein.* Bushy den. *Clumhach,* rough, hairy, bushy; *dein,* den. Mh had become bh, both being sounded v, and h had been lost. The interchange of b and m is of frequent occurrence. Clubach had become Clubbie.

COAL BURN. Hill Burn. *Coill,* hill.

COATS, COATES. Small fold. *Cuitan,* diminutive of *cuit,* fold. An by mistake had been made s and es instead of ie.

COATES HALL. Coates represents *Cuitan,* small fold, with an made s by mistake instead of ie. Hall is sometimes a proprietor's mansion house, and sometimes a farm house with a large kitchen open to all the workers on the farm.

COBINSHAW. Wood in a hollow. *Cobhan,* hollow; shaw (English), wood, bushy place.

COCK RIG, COCKRIG. Slope on a hill. *Ruigh,* slope, *cnoc,* hill.

COCK RIG END, for *Ruighean Cnoc.* Narrow sloping band along the foot of a hill. *Ruighean,* diminutive of *ruigh,* slope; *cnoc,* hill.

COCKBRIDGE, for Burn Bridge. *Coileach* means both burn and cock, and by mistake the second meaning had been substituted for the first.

COCKBURN. Hill burn. *Cnoc,* hill.

COCKLAW. Hill. *Cnoc,* hill; *lamh,* hill.

COCKLEROW, for Cock Hill Row. Row of houses on a hillside. *Cnoc* (n silent), hill.

COCKMOOR, COCKMUIR Hill moor. *Cnoc,* hill.

COCKMYLANE, for *Cnoc Aillean.* Little hill. *Cnoc,* hill, *aillean,* diminutive of *aill,* hill.

COCKPEN. Hill. *Cnoc,* hill; *beinn,* hill. The second part had been added to explain the corrupted form of the first.

COCKUM WATER. Burn of the little hill. *Cnocan,* diminutive of *cnoc,* hill. *Cnoc* lost n and an became um.

COLDHAME, for *Cul Thom.* Back of the hill. *Cul,* back, *thom, tom* aspirated, hill. T is silent.

COLDWELL, for *Cul Bhaile.* Back town. *Cul,* back, north side; *bhaile, baile* aspirated, town. Bh is equal to w, and *bhaile* had become well. D is a euphonic intrusion.

COLDWELL STRAND. River valley at a town on the back of a hill. *Srathan,* diminutive of *srath,* valley; *cul,* back, *bhaile, baile* aspirated, town. D had been added to an. Bh is equal to w, and *bhaile* had been first waile and then well.

COLDWELLS, for *Bhaile Cul.* Place on the back of a hill. *Bhaile baile* aspirated, farm town, *cul*, back, north. *Bhaile* is pronounced waile, which had become well, and s had been added for euphony Euphonic d had been added to l of *cul.*

COLEGATE Hill road. *Coill*, hill; gate (English), road

COLINTON, for *Baile Coillean.* Town at a little hill. *Baile,* town; *coillean*, diminutive of *coille*, hill.

COLTBRIDGE. Bridge over a small burn. *Coilteach*, strengthened form of *coileach*, small burn. Ch with its preceding vowels had been lost.

COLTON DEAN. Den of the little hill. *Coilltean*, diminutive of *coill*, hill, *dein*, den.

COLZIUM. Little hill. *Coillean*, diminutive of *coill*, hill.

COMBFOOT Common fold in which several persons had a joint right. *Comh-chuit* Joint fold. *Comh*, common, *chuit*, *cuit* aspirated, fold. Mh being often silent it had been strengthened by b, and ch had become ph, which is equal to f

COMELY BANK. Bank where assemblies were held. *Coimhlin*, assembly. H had been lost, and in had abnormally become y

COMELY RIG, for *Ruigh Coimhlin* Hillside of the assembly. *Ruigh*, slope near the base of a hill *coimhlin*, assembly. In had abnormally become y

COMISTON. Town held jointly. *Coimeas*, co-equal.

COMMON, COMMON HILL. Pasture ground to which several persons had an equal right, shieling. Communitas (Latin), joint right.

COMPASS SLACK. Place in a howe between a burn and a tributary. *Camas*, point between two burns, *slochd*, howe P had been inserted after m.

CORBIES CRAIG, CORBY LIN, CORBYHALL, CORBYHILL. Corbies and Corby were originally *Chuitail*, *cuitail* aspirated, fold, which was corrupted into whitehill and turned again into Gaelic by *corban*, white hill (*cor*, hill, *ban*, white) Craig is *creag*, hill; lin is *linne*, waterfall, hall is a farm house, and hill is *coill*, hill, translated.

CORDLEAN. Level-topped hill. *Cor*, round hill, *lean*, plain, Euphonic d had been added to cot

CORNBANK. Level terrace on a hillside. *Carn*, hill.

CORNTON Hill town. *Carn*, hill.

CORSTON Town at a place where a hill was crossed. *Cross*, crossing

CORSTORPHINE. Round steep hill. *Cor*, round hill, with s added for euphony, *torr*, round, steep, flat-topped hill, *fin*, hill.

CORTLEFERRY Ferry at a round knoll. *Cor*, round hill; *tulach*, round knoll.

COTLY HILL. Hill of the fold *Lamh* (mh silent), hill, *cuit*, fold.

COTTIE HILL. Hill of the small fold. *Cuiton uian* fold. An normally became ie

COTTYBURN. Burn of the little fold. *Cuitan*, diminutive of *cuit*, fold. An normally passed into y in Scotch.

COUSLAND, for *Lamhan Cobhan*. Hillock in a hollow. *Lamhan*, little hill; *cobhan*, hollow. Mh in *lamhan* is silent, and d had been added for euphony. Bh in *cobhan* is equal to u, and an had improperly been changed to s.

Cow BRIDGE. Bridge at a fold. *Cuith*, fold. Th being silent had been lost. ·

COWBRAEHILL. Hill of the fold. *Braigh*, hill; *cuith* (th silent), fold.

COWDENBOG. Bog in a den in which there was a fold. *Bog*, wet soft place; *dein*, den; *cuith* (th silent), fold.

COWHILL. Hill of the fold. *Cuith* (th silent), fold. Cow had been pronounced coo till recently.

COWPITS for *Pettan Cuith*. Small farm at a fold. *Pettan*, small farm; *cuith* (th silent), fold. An should have become ie, not s.

COWTHROPLE, for *Cuith Ruigh Poll*. Fold on a hill slope near a pool. *Cuith*, fold; *ruigh*, slope; *poll*, pool, burn.

CRAIG, CRAIGBANK, CRAIG WOOD, CRAIGCROOK. Craig is *creag*, hill; crook is *cnoc*, hill. *Cnoc* is in some places pronounced croc or crochg.

CRAIGEND HILL, CRAIGENGAR, CRAIGENTERRIE, CRAIGENTINNIE, CRAIGIEHALL. The first part of the names represents *Creagan*, small hill; gar is *gobhar*, goat; terrie is *tirean*, small bit of arable ground; tinnie is *teine*, fire; and hall is *choill*, *coill* aspirated, hill.

CRAIGLEITH, CRAIGLOCKHART, CRAIGMILLAR, CRAIGO'ER, CRAIG-ROYSTON. The first part of the names is *Creag*, hill; leith is *leith*, side; lockhart is *loch ard*, loch of the hill; millar is *meall airidh*, hill of the shieling; o'er is *gobhar*, goat; royston is *rustan*, little hill

CRAIGS, for *Creagan*. Small hill, or hills. *Creagan* may be either the diminutive or the plural of *creag*, hill.

CRAIGSIDE. Side of a cliff. *Creag*, cliff, rock, hill.

CRAMOND. Moor of the fold. *Monadh*, moor, *cra*, fold made of wattles. For sheep slender rods were plaited together, for cattle stems of trees were split and the parts were planted in the ground obliquely so that they crossed one another twice or thrice as the legs of the letter x do.

CRANSTON. Town at a tree. *Crann*, tree.

CRANSTON EDGE. Brae of Cranston. *Aod*, brae, brow of a hill. See Cranston.

CRAW HILL. Hill of the fold. *Cra*, wattled fold.

CRAWLEY. Grass-land at a fold. *Cra*, fold, ley (Scotch), grassy place.

CREW. Fold. *Crubh* (Irish), fold, fank, cruive.

CRIBBIELAW, Hill of the long narrow ridge. *Lamh*, hill; *cribean*, diminutive of *crib*, comb, sharp long ridge.

CRICHTON. Hill town. *Creach*, hill.

CROFT AN RIGH. Croft on the slope of a hill. *Croit*, croit ; *an*, of the , *ruigh*, slope near the base of a hill

CROFTHEAD. Croft at a fold. *Croit*, croft, hump ; *chuid*, *cuid* aspirated, fold C silent had been dropped.

CROMLIX. Circle of stones. *Crom*, circle , *leacan*, genitive plural of *leac*, stone slab An became s in passing into Scotch, and c and s made x. There had been at Cromlix a circle of stone pillars round a pre-Christian grave

CROMSIDE, for *Suidhe Cruim*. Place of the circle. *Suidhe*, place ; *cruim*, genitive of *crom*, circle, fold.

CROMWELL'S WIT Cromwell's is for *Baile Crom*. Town at a fold. *Baile*, town ; *crom*, circle, fold *Baile* had been put last and made *bhaile*, pronounced waile, and afterwards well S had been added to make an English possessive. Wit represents *chuit*, *cuit* aspirated, fold, in which ch, being silent, had been lost, and uit had become wit. The name Cromwell's Wit does not refer to Oliver Cromwell.

CROOKED RIG, for *Cnocan Ruigh*. Little hill. *Cnocan*, diminutive of *cnoc*, hill ; *ruigh*, hill, slope. Both parts of the name mean hill.

CROOKS. Small hill. *Cnocan*, diminutive of *cnoc*, hill. *Cnoc* in most places is sounded croc or crochg An ought to have become ie, but by mistake it had been made s. This added to croc made crocs, now crooks.

CROOKSTON Hill town. *Cnoc*, hill, with s added to obtain an English possessive.

CROOKSTONE Stone on a hill. *Cnoc* (pronounced croc), hill

CROSS SWARD, for *Crois Sugach Ard*. Crossing over a wet hill *Crois*, crossing , *sughach*, wet , *ard*, height, hill.

CROSSLEE. Grass-land at a crossing. *Crois*, cross , *ley* (Scotch), level grassy place

CROW, CROW HILL, CROW MOSS. In these names Crow represents *cro*, fold made of wattles.

CRUMBLANDS. Crooked hill. *Crom*, crooked , *lamhan*, diminutive of *lamh*, hill An had been regarded as a plural instead of a diminutive termination.

CRUNZIAN. Small round hill. *Cruinnean*, diminutive of *cruinne*, roundness.

CUDDY BRIDGE. Bridge at a small fold. *Cuidan*, diminutive of *cuid*, fold. An had normally become y.

CUIKEN. Little hill. *Cnuican*, diminutive of *cnoc*, hill The diminutive had been formed from the genitive *cnuic*, instead of the nominative

CULLEN. Little burn *Coileachan* (ch silent), little burn.

CUNNIGAR. Hill in which rabbits burrow. *Coinniceir* (Irish), rabbit burrow.

CURRIE. Bog. *Currach*, marsh, bog

CURRIE LEE. Grassy place at a small farm town. *Curra*, small farm ; *ley* (Scotch), grassy loan at a house.

CUSHIE SYKE, for *Alltan Cuaiche*. Little burn from a cup-shaped howe. *Alltan*, little burn, syke; *cuaiche*, genitive of *cuach*, cup.

DALHOUSIE. Field abounding in hollows. *Dail*, field; *chosach*, *cosach* aspirated, abounding in hollows.

DALKEITH. Field at a fold *Dail*, field, *cuith*, fold

DALMAHOY, for *Dail na Chuith*. Field of the fold. *Dail*, field; *na*, of the; *chuith*, *cuith* aspirated, fold. C being silent in ch had been lost. Final th is silent and had been lost.

DALMORE. Big field *Dal*, field; *mor*, big.

DALRY, for *Dail Ruigh*. Field on the lower slope of a hill. *Dail*, field; *ruigh*, slope where cultivation begins.

DANDERHALL. Meaning uncertain. Perhaps Hill of judgment on a shieling *Choill*, *coill* aspirated, hill; *dan*, seat of judgment, *airidh*, shieling Courts were held to settle disputes about shielings and mosses in which several persons were concerned.

DARCY. Bright. *Dearsach*, beaming, radiant.

DARMEAD LINN. Burn of great size. *Linne*, burn, pool, waterfall; *dear* (Irish), great; *mead*, size.

DAVIDSON'S MAINS The origin of this name is obscure. Mains represents Terra Dominicalis (Latin), part of an estate cultivated by the proprietor. Dominicalis passing through French became domains, now mains.

DEAD BURN. Black burn *Dubh*, black.

DEAFLAW HILL. Black hill. *Dubh*, black; *lamh*, hill.

DEAN. Valley excavated by running water. *Dein*, den.

DEAN BRIDGE. Bridge over a den. *Dein*, den.

DEANHEAD. Head of a dean or den. Or, Fold in a den. *Dein*, den; *chuid*, *cuid* aspirated, fold; c in ch being silent had been lost.

DEDRIDGE. Beautiful slope. *Deadh*, fair, beautiful; *ruigh*, slope at the base of a hill.

DELF WELL, for *Dail Phuill*. Field of the pool. *Dail*, field; *phuill*, genitive aspirated of *poll*, pool, river.

DENHAM. Town in a den. Ham (Frisian), hamlet; *dein*, den.

DEWAR GILL. Glen of the black shiel. Gill, glen, *dubh*, black; *airidh*, shiel, hut on summer pasture among hills.

DOBIE'S KNOWE. Black Knoll. *Dubh*, black. S had been inserted to produce the English possessive.

DOD HILL. Hill. Hill is a translation of dod, a corruption of *cnoc*, hill.

DODRIDGE Law Dodridge is for *Ruigh Cnoc*, slope of the hill (*ruigh*, slope; *cnoc*, hill). Law is *lamh*, hill, added to explain dod, a corruption of *cnoc*.

DOG BUSH KNOWE. Knoll of the black wood. *Dubh*, black. Bh had become gh, and h had been lost.

DOVERIDGE. Black slope. *Dubh*, black, *ruighe*, slope at the base of a hill.

DOVITSHILL. Hill of the black region Dovits may be *dubh aite*, black place (*dubh*, black ; *aite*, place), with s added to obtain a possessive. Final e is usually lost.

DOW CRAIG WOOD. Wood of the black hill. *Dubh*, black ; *creag*, hill.

DOWIES MILL If the name is old it may originally have been *Muileann Dubhach*, black mill, mill built of black sods (*muileann*, mill , *dubhach*, black) Bh would become ow, and ach would become ie Final s had been added to make Dowie possessive.

DOWNIE PLACE. Place of a little hill. *Dunan*, little hill. An became ie

DREGHORN. Hill of the hawthorn *Draighionn*, hawthorn ; *carn*, hill C of *carn* had become ch, which had been changed to th, and then t being silent had been dropped

DRESSELRIG, for *Dreasail Ruigh*. Slope of a hill where brambles or thorns grow *Dreasail*, thorny, growing brambles ; *ruigh*, slope of a hill

DROVE LOAN. Green road through a moor for driving cattle to shielings and to markets. Loan (English), grassy lane. Loan in Scotch is a grassy place before a house.

DRUIDICAL CIRCLE John Aubrey, an antiquarian patronised by Charles II , promulgated his belief that stone circles were Druidical places of worship This theory has now died out, and they are regarded as guarding places where pagan interments had been made.

DRUM Long ridge *Druim*, ridge of a hill

DRUM HAGS. Moss holes on a long hill. *Druim*, ridge , hag (Scotch), pot in a moss.

DRUMBRYDON. Hill *Druim*, long ridge, *bruch*, hill , *dun*, hill.

DRYBURN, DRYDEN, DRYLAND. Dry is for *Draigh*, thorntree , land is *lamh*, hill.

DUDDINGSTON Black hill town. *Dubh*, black , *dun*, hill Un in *dun* had been regarded as a plural termination, and s had been added to ng.

DUN LAW. Hill. *Dun* hill ; *lamh*, hill.

DUNARD. Height. *Dun*, hill , *ard*, height.

DUNCLIFFE. Cliff of a hill. *Dun*, hill . cliff (English), steep side of a hill

DUNEDIN. Brae of the hill *Aodann*, brae ; *dun*, hill

DUNESK. Hill of the river. *Dun*, hill , *uisge*, water, river.

DUNSAPIE. Hill of retreat. *Dun*, hill , *seapach*, retreating. In times of danger from thieves the cattle pasturing on Arthur's Seat had been driven to Dunsapie

DYKER LAW, for *Lamh Dubh Airidh* Hill of the black shieling. *Lamh*, hill ; *dubh*, black , *airidh*, shieling

EDGE, EDGEFIELD, EDGEHEAD, EDGELAW. Edge in these names represents *aod*, brae, hill D is often sounded as dg Head is *chuid*, *cuid* aspirated, fold, with silent c lost ; law is *lamh*, hill, with mh sounded as w

EDGEHILL. Fold. Originally *Chuitail*, *cuitail* aspirated, fold, which had been corrupted into whitehill. This had afterwards been turned into Gaelic by *aodgeal*, white hill. *Aod* is pronounced with a long and o silent, and g in *geal* became soft and united with d of *aod*. This produced Edgehill, which in other places has become Aigle, Adziel, Eagle, Eccle, and Edzell.

EDINBURGH. Brae of the hill. *Aodann*, brae; *bruch*, hill. Auld Reekie (High Street) means steep slope. *Alt* (Irish), high place; *ruighe*, slope.

EDMONSTONE, for *Aod Baile Maise*. Brae of the beautiful farm town. *Aod*, brae; *baile*, town; *maise*, beauty. See Meston.

ELDIN, for *Aill Dun*. Both parts mean hill. *Aill*, hill; *dun*, hill.

ELDRICK, for *Ruigh Aill*. Slope of a hill. *Ruigh*, slope, shieling, hill; *aill*, hill. The parts had been transposed to avoid a hiatus.

ELF LOCH. Loch of the hill. Elf is an abbreviation of *aillfin* (*aill*, hill; *fin*, hill), and it is wrongly supposed to mean a fairy or spirit.

ELGINHAUGH. Haugh at a hill of sand. *Aill*, hill; *gaineamh*, sand. Mh and its antecedent vowels had been lost.

ELLEN'S BURN. Burn of the green plain. *Ailean*, green plain.

EMLY BANK. Bank on the side of a stream. *Amhainn*, river; *leth* (th silent), side. Ainn had become ie, which had been lost. Th final is silent and had been lost.

ENGLAND'S HILL. The Hill. England's represents *An Lamhan*, The Hill. *An*, the; *lamhan*, hill. Mh is silent and had been lost. D is frequently added to n. S was added to make England possessive.

ENTERKIN'S YETT, for *Chuit an Tir Ceann*. Fold at the head of the land. *Chuit*, *cuit* aspirated, fold; *an*, of the; *ceann*, head; *tir*, land. Ch of *chuit* became gh, equal to y. Ann had been regarded as a plural termination and had been made s.

ESHERVILLE. If this name is of Gaelic origin it represents *Eas Airidh Mhill* and means burn of the shieling on a hill. *Eas* (pronounced esh), burn; *airidh*, shieling; *mhill* (pronounced vil), genitive aspirated of *meall*, hill.

ESK. Running water. *Uisge*, water, stream.

ESPERSTON. Town consisting of a row of houses at a burn. *Eas*, burn; *peirse*, row.

EWES CASTLE. Guard house at a small fold. *Chuithan*, *cuithan* aspirated, small fold. Ch and th becoming silent had been lost, and an had been made es instead of ie. The castle had been a shelter for those who watched the fold at night.

FAIRAFAR. Hill of the cultivated ground. *Fair*, hill, ridge; *a'*, of the; *far* cultivated land.

FAIRHOPE. Hill. *Fair*, hill; *chop*, *cop* aspirated, hill. C in ch is silent and had been lost.

FAIRMILEHEAD, for *Fair Meall Chuid*. Hill of the cattlefold. *Fair*, hill, *meall*, hill; *chuid*, *cuid* aspirated, fold. C in ch is silent and had been lost. The first two parts have the same meaning

FALA, FALA HILL, FALA KNOWE, FALA LUGGIE. Fala is *falamh* (mh silent), uncultivated land, luggie is *lughaidh*, smallness, small.

FALA FLOW, FALA FLOW LOCH. Pool on Fala Moor. Flow represents *flodh*, a variant of *plodh*, pool, loch

FALL HILLS. Hills. *Choill*, *coill* aspirated, hill Ch became f.

FATLIPS, for *Luban Chat*. Little bend in a road. *Luban* diminutive of *lub*, bend; *chat*, *cat* aspirated, road Ch had become ph which is f.

FAUCH HILL. Hill whereof some part had been ploughed. Fauch (Scotch), to plough

FEATHER HALL. Mansion at a burn passing through a shieling *Feith*, moss burn. *airidh*, shieling Hall originally meant the great room in a castle, free to all the residents, now it often means a mansion which has taken the place of a castle.

FERNIE GRAIN Ferny place between two branches of a burn. Grain is the same as groin

FERNIEFLAT. Level place growing ferns.

FERNIEHIRST. Bushy place growing ferns Huist (English), wood.

FETTES, for *Chuidan*. Small fold. *Chuitan*, *cuitan* aspirated, diminutive of *cuit*, fold. Ch became ph, which is equal to f, and an, being erroneously regarded as a plural termination, became es instead of ie Fuites lapsed into fettes.

FILLYSIDE, for *Suidhe Feille*. Site of a market. *Suidhe*, site, *feille*, genitive of *feill*, market, festival.

FIRTH, for *Thriath* Hill. *Thriath*, *triath* aspirated, hill. Th became ph, equal to f.

FIRTH OF FORTH Estuary near an enclosed place. *Chorth*, *corth* aspirated, enclosed place, fold, fort.

FIVE HOUSES. Houses at a fold *Chuith*, *cuith* aspirated, fold. Ch had become ph or f, and th had become ch or v.

FLOTTERSTONE. Stone on a wet shieling. *Fliuch*, wet; *airidh*, shieling.

FORDEL Field in front of a hill. *For*, before; *dail*, field.

FOUL SLUSH, for *Pholl Slios*. Burn on a hillside. *Pholl*, *poll* aspirated, pool, burn, *slios*, hillside.

FOWIE, for *Chuithan*. Small fold *Chuithan*, *cuithan* aspirated, small fold. Ch became ph or f, th became bh or w, and an became ie. Sometimes euphonic l is inserted in fowie, making it fowlie.

FREELANDS, for *Lamhan Threith* Both parts mean hill. *Lamhan*, diminutive of *lamh*, hill; *threith*, genitive aspirated of *triath*, hill In *lamhan* mh being silent had been lost, and an, had improperly been made s. Th in *threith* had become ph, which is f, and final th being silent had been lost

C

FRIARTON, for *Baile Thriath*. Town on a hill. *Baile*, town , *thriath*, *triath* aspirated, hill.

FUFFET, for *Chuith Chuit*. Both parts mean fold. The aspirated letters became ph or f, which produced fuffuit.

FULFORD, for *Ath Phuill*. Ford over a burn. *Ath*, ford ; *phuill*, genitive aspirated of *poll*, pool, burn. In names *poll* usually means burn. Ph is equal to f.

FULLARTON. Town at a burn from a hill. *Poll*, burn ; *ard*, hill. P had become ph or f.

FUMART SYKE. Drain from a fold for cows. *Chuith*, *cuith* aspirated, fold ; *mart*, cow. Ch had become ph or f, and th silent had been lost.

FUSHIE, for *Chuith Sith*. Fold on a hill. *Chuith*, *cuith* aspirated, fold ; *sith*, hill. Ch had become ph, equal to f, and th is silent. *Sith* is pronounced she.

GALA WATER. Gala had originally been *Cuit*, fold, corrupted into white and turned again into Gaelic by *gealach*, white. The name Gala Water therefore means water passing a fold.

GALACHLAW, GALALAW. Fold. *Chuitail*, *cuitail* aspirated, fold ; *lamh*, hill. *Chuitail* became whitehill, which was turned into Gaelic by *gealachlamh*, white hill (*gealach*, white ; *lamh*, hill).

GALLADALE. White field. *Gealach*, white , *dail*, field near a river. *Galla* had originally been *chuit*, *cuit* aspirated, fold, which had been corrupted into white, and turned again into Gaelic by *gealach*, white.

GARVAL SYKE. Rough burn syke. *Garbh*, rough ; *allt*, burn.

GARVALD. Rough burn. *Garbh*, rough ; *allt*, burn.

GASK HILL. Hill on a narrow point. *Gasg*, tail, long narrow strip of land.

GATELY RIG. Windy slope. *Gaothlach*, variant of *gaothach*, windy ; *ruigh*, slope of a hill.

GAVIESIDE, for *Suidhe Gabhann*. Site of a fold. *Suidhe*, place ; *gabhann*, fold. Ann had become ie.

GILDYHOWES. Originally *Chuit Tollan*. Fold in a little howe. *Chuit*, *cuit* aspirated, fold ; *tollan*, little howe. *Chuit* was corrupted into white, and white was again turned into Gaelic by *gilide* (Irish), whiteness, white.

GILLYGUB DEAN. Den of the fir tree at the fold. Gilly had originally been *Chuit*, *cuit* aspirated, fold, which had been corrupted into white, and turned again into Gaelic by *gealach*, white. Gub represents *giubhas*, fir-tree ; and dean is the English word meaning den.

GILMERTON, for *Chuit Baile Mor*. Fold at a big town. *Chuit*, *cuit* aspirated, fold ; *baile*, town ; *mor*, big. *Chuit* had been corrupted into white, which had again been turned into Gaelic by *geal*, white.

GILSTON. Town at a small ravine. *Gill*, small burn, valley.

GLADHOUSE. If this name is Gaelic it must mean protected fold. *Gleidhte*, protected ; *chuith*, *cuith* aspirated, fold. C silent had been lost, and th had become sh, with subsequent loss of h.

GLADSMUIR. Moor of the kite. *Glede* (English), kite.

GLASSMAN'S SIKE. Drain from a green hill *Glas*, green, *man*, hill.

GLEDE KNOWE. Knoll over which kites often hovered in quest of mice, beetles, &c. *Glede* (English), kite.

GLEN BROOK. Glen of the hill *Gleann*, glen ; *bruch*, hill.

GLENCORSE, GLENCROSS Glen crossing a hill range. *Gleann*, glen , *craisg*, crossing

GLENDARACH. Glen of oaks. *Gleann*, glen , *darach*, oak-tree.

GLENHUTCH. Glen of the fold *Gleann*, glen ; *chuith*, *cuith* aspirated, fold C m ch is silent and had been lost Huith had been strengthened by the insertion of c.

GLENTRESS. Glen of the hill. *Gleann*, glen , *triath*, hill. Th had become sh, and h had afterwards been lost.

GOGAR Fold on a shieling. *Gog*, fold , *airidh* (idh silent), shieling

GOODTREES, for *Cuid Triath*. Fold on a hill *Cuid*, fold , *triath*, hill

GORBALS, for *Bailean Gorth*. Little town at a fold *Bailean*, diminutive of *baile*, town , *gorth* (th silent), fold Ean had been made s instead of ie. The accent on the first syllable shows that the parts of the name had been transposed Final th is silent.

GORE WATER. Water on whose banks goats fed *Gobhar*, goat.

GOREBRIDGE. Bridge for goats. *Gobhar*, goat. Bh is silent.

GORGIE, for *Goirtean*. Small enclosure. *Goirtean*, diminutive of *gort*, enclosure, stone circle round a grave, fold, garden. The soft sound of g results from sounding e as y. An normally became ie

GORTONLEE Grass-land at a small fold *Gortan*, diminutive of *gort*, circle, fold , ley (Scotch), grassy place. *Gortan* has usually become Gordon

GOURLAW. Hill of the goats. *Lamh*, hill ; *gobhar*, genitive plural of *gobhar*, goat.

GOWANBRAE. Daisy brae. Gowan represents *Gabhann*, fold made with posts set into the ground in a circle, which the flower of the daisy resembles. Bh is equivalent to u, v, or w.

GOWANHILL Cattle-fold hill. *Gabhann*, fold. Bh is equal to w.

GOWKHILL. Hill. *Cnoc*, hill. The second part is a translation of the first.

GOWKLIE MOSS. Hillside moss. *Cnoc*, hill ; *leth* (th silent), side Gowk is pronounced with the vocal organs nearly in the same position as for *cnoc*

GRACEMOUNT. If this is an old name it means in prosperity, good fortune. *Grais*, good luck ; *moradi*, m ·

GRAIN HILL. Meaning uncertain. If the hill is covered with grass the name may mean green hill. If exposed to the south and sheltered from the north it may mean sunny, coming from *grian*, sun. ' If the hill is composed of sand the name may represent *grainneach*, sandy.

GRANGE. Farm house on land owned and occupied by a monastery. Grange (Old French), barn, granary.

GRANTON, for *Grant Dun*. Green hill. *Grant* (Irish), green ; *dun*, hill.

GRAVES KNOWES. Rough Knolls. *Garbh*, rough.

GRAY BRAE. Hill. *Creag*, hill ; *braigh*, hill.

GREAT LAW. Hill. *Creach*, hill ; *lamh*, hill.

GREEN LAW, GREENHALL. Green hill. Law is for *lamh* (mh equal to w), hill ; hall is for *choill, coill* aspirated, hill, in which c silent had been lost, leaving hoill, now hall.

GREYKNOWE. Grey is a corruption of *creag*, hill, and knowe is a translation of *creag*.

GREYSTONE HEAD. Fold at a stone on a hill. *Chuid, cuid* aspirated, fold ; *creag*, hill. C in ch is silent and had been lost.

GREYSTONE KNOWE. Knoll of the rock. *Creag*, rock. Stone is a translation of *creag*.

GRIM BRIGS, GRIM HAVEN. Grim represents *grimeach*, rugged, grim. Brigs represents *bruchan*, little hill An had been made s instead of ie.

GROATHILL. Hill of the fold. *Crotha*, genitive of *cro*, fold. Final vowels in names are often lost.

GUIDE ABOUT, for *Cuid a' Buth*. Fold at a shiel. *Cuid*, fold, *a*, of the ; *buth*, hut, house on a shieling.

GUNS GREEN. Grassy place at a fold. *Gabhann*, fold. Bh is equal to u. S had been added because ann had been regarded as a plural termination.

GUTTED HADDIE. Brae where corn was winnowed. *Aodann*, brae ; *guiteach*, winnowing. There was formerly cultivated land far up Arthur's Seat. Ann normally became ie.

GUTTERFORD, for *Ath Cuit Airidh*. Ford at a fold on a shieling. *Ath*, ford ; *cuit*, fold ; *airidh*, shieling.

HABBIES HOWE. Howe eaten out by running water. *Chaobta*, past participle aspirated of *caob*, to bite. C in ch is silent and had been lost.

HADFAST, for *Achadh Fas* Desolate land. *Achadh*, place, *fas*, waste.

HAG BRAE, for *Braigh Agh*. Hill of joy. *Braigh*, hill ; *agh*, joy, happiness. The parts of the name had been transposed to avoid a hiatus. Then h had been prefixed to *agh*.

HAGGS. Holes in mosses where peats have been dug.

HAGIERAE, for *Rath Aghann*. Circle of the fold. *Rath*, circle ; *aghann*, fold, with ann made ie.

HAILES. Green plain. *Ailean*, level green place. H had been prefixed to facilitate pronunciation, and an had been made s instead of ie.

HALA SHANK, for *Sithean Fhala*. Hill of the moor. *Sithean* (pronounced shan), hill, *fhala, fala* aspirated, genitive of *fal*, moor, pasture. Euphonic k has been added to n, and f in fh had been lost, being silent

HALFLAW KILN, for *Coill Lamh Coillean*. Hill. *Coill*, hill, *lamh*, hill; *coillean*, diminutive of *coill*, hill, *Coill* had been made *choill*, then c had been lost, and f had been inserted

HALK LAW. Hawk hill. *Lamh*, hill.

HALL CRAIGS. Both parts mean hill. *Choill, coill* aspirated, hill; *creagan* diminutive of *creag*, hill. C in *choill* is silent and had been lost. An of *creagan* had been made s instead of ie. In old Gaelic *coill* means hill

HALL LISTON. Hill at Liston. *Choill, coill* aspirated, hill. C silent had been lost.

HALLHERIOT. Hill of the shieling. *Choill, coill* aspirated, hill; *airidh*, shieling, summer pasture among hills

HALLTREE. Both parts mean hill. *Choill, coill* aspirated, hill, *triath*, hill. C in ch and th final had been dropped, being silent.

HALLS. Little hill. *Choillean, coillean* aspirated, little hill. Ean had by mistake been made s instead of ie

HALLYARDS, for *Choill Ardan*. Hill. *Choill, coill* aspirated, hill, *ardan*, little height. C in ch had been lost, and an had been made s instead of ie.

HANDAXWOOD Wood at the head of a field *Cheann, ceann* aspirated, head; *achadh*, field.

HANGING CRAIG, HANGING ROCK, HANGING SHAW. If Hanging is an English word it means sloping or overhanging If it is of Gaelic origin it represents *fhangan*, sheepfold. *Fhangan, fangan* aspirated, little fold. Craig is *creag*, hill; and shaw is a bushy place. F in fh is silent and it had been lost.

HANLEY. Grassy gentle slope. *Fhan, fan* aspirated, gentle slope; ley (Scotch), grassy place F in fh had been lost, being silent Ley might be *lamh* (mh silent), hill

HANNAHFIELD. Field on the slope of a hill. *Fhanadh, fanadh* aspirated, gentle slope. F in fh is usually silent, and often both f and h are lost.

HARBOUR HILL. Hill of the shieling for cattle. *Airidh*, shieling; *buar*, cattle.

HARBURN. Burn of the shieling. *Airidh*, shieling.

HARBURNHEAD. Head of the shieling burn; but head might represent *chuid, cuid* aspirated, fold, in which c is silent.

HARD LAW. Hill. *Ard*, hill, *lamh*, hill

HARDEN GREEN. Green place on a small hill. *Ardan*, diminutive of *ard*, height. H had been prefixed to a for euphony.

HARE CRAIG, HARE HILL, HAREBURN, HAREHOPE, HARELAW, HAREWOOD. Hare is *airidh*, shieling, summer pasture, with euphonic h prefixed, craig is *creag*, hill, hope is *chop, cop* aspirated, hill, with c silent dropped; law is *lamh*, hill, h mh made w.

HARKEN BURN. Burn from the head of the shieling. *Ceann*, head ; *airidh*, shieling.

HARLE RIGGING, for *Airidh Aill Ruighean*. The oldest part of the name is *Aill Ruighean*. Hill of the shieling. *Aill*, hill ; *ruighean*, small shieling. After the meaning of the name had almost been forgotten *airidh*, shieling, had been prefixed to explain it, and h had been put before a for euphony.

HARPER RIG, HARPERS HALL. Harper is a corruption of *airidh*, shieling, to which euphonic h had been prefixed. Rig is *ruigh*, slope ; and hall is *choill, coill* aspirated, hill. Dh of *airidh* had become ph, and h had been dropped.

HARRY'S MUIR. Muir of the shieling. *Airidh*, shieling, with h prefixed.

HARTWOOD. Wood on a hill. *Ard*, hill.

HARVIESTON. Town of the shieling. *Airidh*, shieling.

HARWOOD. Wood of the shieling. *Airidh*, shieling.

HATTON. Small fold. *Chuitan, cuitan* aspirated, diminutive of *cuit*, fold. C being silent in ch had been lost, and huitan had lasped into hatton.

HAWKSTER GILL, for *Gill Osda*. Glen of the inn. *Gill*, glen ; *osda*, inn.

HAY LODGE. Hay, if a place-name, represents *chuith, cuith* aspirated, fold. C in *chuith* is silent, th also is silent, and hui had become hey, the Scotch way of pronouncing hay. But Hay may be a personal name originally given to a person coming from a fold.

HAYMAINS, for *Chuidh Main*. Fold on a hill. *Chuidh, cuidh* aspirated, fold ; *main*, second form of *man*, hill. C in ch is silent, and dh is equal to y. Ain had been regarded as a plural termination, and s had been added to main.

HEAT HILL. Hill of the fold. *Coill*, hill ; *chuit, cuit* aspirated, fold. C in ch had been lost.

HEATHERY BURN. Burn of the fold on the shieling. *Chuith, cuith* aspirated, fold ; *airidh*, shieling.

HEBERSHAW. Shepherd's woods. *Chibeir, cibeir* aspirated, shepherd.

HECKLE BURN. Burn of the place on a hill. *Achadh*, place ; *aill*, hill. H was prefixed to *achadh* for euphony, and dh with its vowel was lost.

HEN MOSS. Moss of the hill. *Fhin, fin* aspirated, hill. In *fhin* f has become silent. Sometimes both f and h are lost, as in Innerwick.

HENDREYS COURSE, for *Crois Fhin Ruigh*. Crossing of the hill of the shieling. *Crois*, crossing ; *fhin, fin* aspirated, hill ; *ruigh*, shieling. F in fh is silent.

HENSHAW. Wood of the hill. *Fhin, fin* aspirated, hill. F in fh is silent and had been lost.

HERIOT. Shieling. *Airidh*, shieling Euphonic h had been prefixed to *airidh*.

HERMAND, for *Monadh Airidh*. Hill of the shieling. *Monadh*, hill , *airidh,* shieling. To avoid a hiatus the parts of the name had been transposed, and for euphony h had been prefixed to *airidh*

HERMISTON. East beautiful town *Air,* east ; *maise,* beauty, attractiveness.

HERRING ROW. Row of houses on a small shieling. *Airidhean,* small shieling. H had been prefixed for euphony

HEWING, for *Chuithan* Small fold *Chuithan, cuithan* aspirated, small fold. C in ch is silent and had been lost Th is also silent and had been lost. An became ing, and so also in the name Ewing, but it remains unchanged in Ewan.

HIGH LEE Grassy place at a fold. *Chuith, cuith* aspirated, fold. C and th being silent had been lost ; ley (Scotch), grassland.

HILLEND HILL Little hill. *Choillean, coillean* aspirated, little hill. C in ch is silent and had been lost, and d had been added to n for euphony.

HIREN DEAN, for *Dein Chirean.* Den of the little ridge. *Dein,* den, dean , *chirean, cirean* aspirated, little ridge.

HIVEY LIN, for *Linne Chuithan* Pool at a small fold. *Linne,* pool , *chuithan, cuithan* aspirated, small fold. C silent was lost, th became bh, equal to v, and an normally became ey

HOGHILL Small hill. *Og,* young, small.

HOLLYCOT. Hill of the fold *Choille, coille* aspirated, hill ; *cuit,* fold.

HOLYROOD. If this name is pre-Christian it represents *Ruigh Choille.* Base of the hill. *Ruigh,* lower slope on a hill ; *choille, coille* aspirated, hill. Gh and dh have the same sound, hence g and d are mistaken for one another C in ch is silent and had been lost. In old Gaelic *coille* means hill ; in modern it means wood. If the name is post-Christian it means holy cross.

HONEY BRAE Hill of meeting. *Braigh,* hill ; *choinne, coinne* aspirated, meeting.

HONEY HOLE, for *Coill Choinne.* Hill of assembly *Coill,* hill , *choinne, coinne* aspirated, meeting. When *choinne* became honey it was put first, and *coill* was made *choill* and put last. C in *choinne* and in *choill* had been lost, being silent.

HONEYWALLS, for *Bailean Choinne.* Little town where assemblies were held. *Bailean,* little town, made *bhailean,* and put last ; *choinne, coinne* aspirated, meeting. Bh is equal to w, and ean had improperly been made s instead of ie, which produced bhails, pronounced walls. C in *choinne,* being silent, had been dropped.

HOPE, HOPE BURN, HOPE RIG, HOPEFIELD. Hope is *chop, cop* aspirated, hill, silent c being lost By the position of some names on the Ordnance Survey maps it seems that Hope was supposed to mean a sheltered place Rig is *ruigh,* slope on a hillside.

HOPPER CLEUGH. Steep bank on the hill of the shieling. *Chop, cop* aspirated, hill ; *airidh,* shieling.

HOPRINGLE. Originally *Chuitail, cuitail* aspirated, fold.

Chuitail was corrupted into whitehill, which was again turned into Gaelic by *ruigheangeal*, white hill (*ruighean*, slope of a hill; *geal*, white). This had been changed to ringle, and then hop for *cop*, hill, had been prefixed, making hopringle, now hoppringle.

HOSELAW, for *Lamh Chois*. Hill of the fold. *Lamh*, hill; *chos*, *cos* aspirated, fold.

HOWATSTONE. Stone at the fold. *Chuit*, *cuit* aspirated, fold. C in ch is silent and had been omitted.

HOWDEN, for *Chuidan*. Small fold. *Chuidan*, *cuidan* aspirated, small fold. C had been lost, being silent, and dan had become den.

HOWGATE. Windy fold. *Chuith*, *cuith* aspirated, fold; *gaothach*, windy. *Chuith* lost its silent letters, c and th, and *gaothach* lost hach, which had become silent.

HOWLISTON. Town at a fold. The oldest part of the name is *lios*, fold, to which had been prefixed *chuith*, *cuith* aspirated, fold, as an explanation. C, being silent, had been lost, and so also had th with its vowels.

HUGGIESHOLE, for *Ugan Choille*. Breast of the hill. *Ugan*, breast; *choille*, *coille* aspirated, hill. For euphony h was prefixed to u; an normally became ie, and it was also improperly made s to obtain a possessive. C in ch was lost, and oi became o.

HUNT LAW. Hill of assembly. *Lamh*, hill; *choinne*, *coinne* aspirated, assembly. Euphonic t had been added to n.

HUNTERFIELD. Place of meeting on a shieling. *Choinne*, *coinne* aspirated, meeting-place; *airidh*, shieling. C in ch is silent.

HUNTLY COT, for *Cuit Tulach Choinne*. Fold on the hill where meetings were held. *Cuit*, fold; *tulach*, hill; *choinne*, *coinne* aspirated, meeting.

HURCHEON. Shieling of the little fold. *Airidh*, shieling; *chuitan*, *cuitan* aspirated, little fold. Euphonic h had been prefixed to a, and idh had been lost. Th being silent had been lost along with antecedent i.

HURLEY. Shieling on a hill. *Airidh*, shieling, with h prefixed; *lamh* (mh silent), hill.

HYVOT'S BANK. Hyvots is for *Chuith Bhothan*. Fold at a small house. *Chuith*, *cuith* aspirated, fold; *bhothan*, *bothan* aspirated, small house. In *chuith* c and th had been lost, being silent. In *bhothan* bh is equal to v, the aspirate in th had been lost, and an had by mistake been made s instead of ie.

INCH. Enclosed place. *Innis*, place enclosed by water, land, fence, hills. It may mean island, lake, garden, fold, stone circle, hollow.

INGLIS GREEN. Green place at the fold. *An* (n nasal), the; *lios*, fold.

INGLISTON, for *Baile an Lios*. Town at the fold. *Baile*, town; *an*, of the; *lios*, fold.

INKS. Fold. *Chuitail*, *cuitail* aspirated, fold, which had been corrupted into whitehill and afterwards turned into Gaelic by *fhincan*, white hill (*jhin*, *fin* aspirated, hill; *can*, white) Fh is often silent and had been lost An had been mistaken for a plural termination and had been made s. Incs is now inks.

INVERESK, for *Inbhir Uisye*. Infall of the Esk. *Inbhir*, infall, *uisge*, water, river Esk.

INVERLEITH. Ford across the water of Leith. *Inbhir*, infall, ford; Leith, stream name, probably a corruption of *luath*, feminine of *luath*, rapid. Bh is equivalent to v.

JANEFIELD Field of the hill. *Sithean* (pronounced shean), hill.

JARG. Red place. *Dearg*, red.

JEANFIELD. Hill field. *Sithean* (pronounced shean), hill

JEFFRIES CORSE, for *Crois Dubh Triath*. Crossing over a black hill. *Crois*, crossing, *dubh*, (d equal to dg) black, *triath*, hill.

JOCK'S CLEUGH. Steep-sided gorge in a howe *Iochd*, howe

JOCK'S LODGE. Lodge in a howe. *Iochd*, howe.

JOHN'S BURN. Burn of the hill *Dun*, hill S had been added to obtain a possessive.

JOPPA BURN. Black burn. *Dubh*, black, *abh*, water.

JORDAN BURN. Burn of the hill *Chor*, cor aspirated, round hill; *dun*, hill.

KAIM, KAIMES, KAIMS Kaim is the Scotch for comb, the crest of a cock The moraines of extinct glaciers, with steep sides and sharp ridges at the top, are called kaims.

KATES MILL. Mill of the small fold. *Cuitan*, diminutive of *cuit*, fold. An should have been made ie and not s.

KAYTHE, KAYTHE CASTLE *Cuith*, fold At some folds guard-houses were built to accommodate men who guarded the folds against cattle-thieves.

KEIRSHILL. Hill with a long sharp ridge on the summit *Cir*, crest, comb. S had been added to Keir to make it an English possessive.

KELLERSTAIN. Stone at the head of the shieling. *Ceann*, head; *airidh*, shieling. The form *cinn* often]takes the place of *ceann*, and sometimes *cinn* becomes cill

KELLY SYKE. Drain from a hill. *Coille*, hill

KENLEITH. Head of the steep side. *Ceann*, head; *leith*, side. *Leith* means the higher of two sides of a burn

KEVOCK Little fold. *Cuithan*, small fold Th had become bh, equal to v, and an had been changed to ock instead of ie, the usual Scotch diminutive.

KILCOUTER. Head of the fold on a shieling. *Cinn* for *ceann*, head; *cuit*, fold; *airidh*, shieling.

KILLANDEAN Narrow place in a den *Caolan*, small narrow place; *dein*, den.

KILLOCHYETT, for *Ceann a' Chuit*. Head of the fold. *Ceann*, head, *a'*, of the; *chuit*, *cuit* aspirated, fold. *Ceann* had assumed the genitive form, *cinn*, which had been softened to cill, now kill.

KILLRIG, for *Ceann Ruigh*. Head of the slope. *Ceann*, head ; *ruigh*, slope at the base of a hill. *Ceann* had taken the genitive form *cinn*, which had become cill and afterwards kill.

KINELLAN. Head of the little hill. *Cinn*, variant of *ceann*, head ; *aillean*, diminutive of *aill*, hill.

KING'S HILL, KING'S HILL HEAD, KING'S KNOWE, KINGS SEAT. King's is for *Ceann*, head, with s added because it ended in ann, thought to be a plural termination. Head is *chuid*, *cuid* aspirated, fold. Seat is for *suidhe*, site, place.

KIP. Head of a hill. *Ceap*, summit.

KIPPIT, for *Cipeag*. Small farm. *Cipeag*, diminutive from *cip*, genitive of *ceap*, plot of ground.

KIPPS, for *Ceapan*, small plot. An had erroneously been regarded as a plural termination.

KIPRIG, for *Ruigh Cip*. Slope of a hill. *Ruigh*, slope ; *cip*, variant of *ceap*, hill.

KIPSYKE. Drain from a small plot of ground. *Ceap*, plot of ground.

KIRKETTLE, for *Creag Cuitail*. Hill of the fold. *Creag*, hill ; *cuitail*, fold. *Creag* often becomes kirk, and sometimes grey.

KIRKHILL. Both parts mean hill. *Creag*, hill. Sometimes this name means hill near a church.

KIRKLAND HILL. The three parts of the name have the same meaning. *Creag*, hill ; *lamhan*, hill. Mh is silent and d had been added to n for euphony.

KIRKLISTON. Church of Liston.

KIRKSHADE. Hill field. *Creag*, hill ; shed (English), division, separated part.

KIRKTON. Hill town. *Creag*, hill. This is the name of a place near Glencross Reservoir.

KITCHEN MOSS. Moss of the little fold. *Cuithan*, small fold. Th had been strengthened by inserting c.

KITCHEN RIG. Little fold on a shieling. *Cuithan*, little fold ; *ruigh*, slope, shieling. C had been inserted between t and h.

KITTYFLAT. Level place at a small fold. *Cuithan*, diminutive of *cuit*, fold. An became y.

KNIGHTFIELD RIG, for *Ruigh Achadh Cnoc*. Slope of the field on the hill. *Ruigh*, slope ; *achadh*, field, place ; *cnoch*, *cnoc* aspirated at the end, hill. Final c of *cnoc* had been aspirated and *cnoch* had been confounded with *cniochd*, knight, soldier.

LADYSIDE, for *Leathan Suidhe*. Broad place. *Leathan*, broad ; *suidhe*, place. Or, for *Leathad*, side, with its translation added. An becomes y in Scotch. In Gaelic final d has often added to it a faint sound of g or y.

LADYWELL. Well dedicated to the Virgin Mary. It had been visited by sick persons, who drank of the water, and by persons with sores, who washed themselves with the water.

LAMMAS BOARD, for *Lamh Maitheas Braid*. Good hill.

Lamh, hill, *maitheas* (pronounced mas), good, goodness, *braid*, hill

LAMMERMUIR   Muir of the shieling hill. *Lamh*, hill; *airidh*, shieling

LANDRIG BURN   Burn from a shieling hill. *Lamhan*, little hill; *ruigh*, shieling, slope on a hill. D is a euphonic insertion.

LANGLAW. Hill   *Lamhan*, little hill; *lamh*, hill. Mh in *lamhan* is silent, but it made an nasal. Mh in *lamh* is equal to w. The second part of the name is an addition made to the first to explain it after it had been corrupted

LANGSIDE. Place on a hill   *Lamhan*, little hill, *suidhe*, place. Mh was lost, being silent, but it made an nasal, and *lamhan* became lang

LANGTON. Hill town. *Lamhan*, diminutive of *lamh*, hill Mh is equal to v but sometimes it is silent and only makes the preceding vowel nasal.

LASSWADE, for *Leas Bhaid.* Fold at a wood. *Leas*, a variant of *lios*, fold; *bhaid*, genitive aspirated of *bad*, wood, bushy place. *Bhaid* is pronounced waid.

LATCH. *Lathach*, mire, wet place in a hollow crossing a road. Th had been strengthened by the insertion of c.

LAUGHATLOTHIAN. Slope of the little side. *Leathad*, declivity; *leordean*, small side, small part of a side.

LAURISTON, for *Baile Ruigh Lamh.* Town on the slope of a hill. *Baile*, town, *ruigh*, shieling, slope, *lamh* (mh silent), hill.

LAWFIELD. Hill field. *Lamh*, hill.

LAWHEAD. Hill of the fold. *Lamh*, hill; *chuid*, *cuid* aspirated, fold. Mh in *lamh* is silent, and c in *chuid* is also silent. Huid had been pronounced heed, now made head.

LAWRIG BURN. Burn on the slope of a hill. *Lamh*, hill, *ruigh*, slope of a hill

LEAD BURN. Broad burn. *Leud*, breadth.

LEASON LAW, for *Lamh Liosan.* Hill of the small fold *Lamh* (mh silent); *liosan* (o silent), diminutive of *lios*, fold.

LEEGATE   Windy grass-land. Ley (Scotch), grass-land; *gaothach*, windy.

LEITH. Stream name   *Luithe*, swiftness, swift

LEITH—WATER OF. Swift river, stream name derived from *luaith*, feminine of *luath*, rapid, or from *luithe*, swiftness, swift

LEITH HEAD MILL. Mill at a fold on the Water of Leith Head is for *Chuid*, *cuid* aspirated, fold. C, being silent, had been lost.

LENNOX TOWER. Tower in a level place   *Liomhanach*, smooth, bright   Mh with its vowels is silent.

LENNY MOOR, for *Moine Leana*   Moor of the plain. *Moine*, moor, *leana*, level plain.

LENNY PORT, for *Port Leana.* Gate in a level plain. *Port*, gate; *leana*, plain.

LEONARDS. If there is no local history connecting this place with a saint named Leonard it may represent *L . . Ardan*, plain of the little height. *Lian*, plain, meadow; *ardan*, diminutive of *ard*, height. An should normally become ie and not s.

LETHAM. Broad place. *Leathan*, broad.

LEVEN HALL, for *Liomhanach Choill*. Smooth hill. *Liomhanach*, smooth; *choill, coill* aspirated, hill.

LEVEN SEAT. Smooth place. *Liomhanach*, smooth, level; *suidhe*, seat, place. Mh is equal to v, and ach had been lost, ch becoming silent.

LIBERTON. Town in a nook of a shieling. *Luib*, bend; *airidh*, shieling.

LINKS, for *Lianan*. Level places near the sea. Final an had normally become s, and c had been inserted for euphony, producing liancs, now links. In Cynewulf's Anglo-Saxon poem "Phoenix", written about 1000 A.D., the word occurs as hlincs; and lincan is in a charter in Reg. Mag. Sig. IV. 479, dated about 1569. Links are ancient sea-beaches, about 25 and 50 feet above sea.

LINN JAW. Black pool. *Linne*, pool; *dubh*, black.

LIN'S MILL. Mill at a waterfall. *Linne*, waterfall, pool.

LISTON. Town at a fold. *Lios* (o silent), fold.

LISTONSHIELS, for *Baile Lios Sealan*. Town at a fold on a shieling. *Baile*, town; *lios*, fold; *sealan*, summer pasture.

LITTLE ELDRICK, for *Ruigh Aill Beag*. Slope of the little hill. *Ruigh*, slope, shieling; *aill*, hill; *beag*, little.

LITTLE FRANCE, for *Beag Threinse*. Little trench. *Beag*, little; *threinse, treinse* aspirated because the adjective precedes the noun, trench. Th had become ph, which is equal to f. The trench is a long aqueduct.

LITTLE VANTAGE. Little fold. Originally Vantage had been *Chuitail, cuitail* aspirated, fold, corrupted into whitehill. This was turned into Gaelic by *bhanaod*, white hill (*bhan, ban* aspirated, white; *aod*, hill, brae). Bh is equal to v, and t is a euphonic addition to n.

LIXMOUNT, for *Monadh Leacan*. Hill of flat stones. *Monadh*, hill; *leacan*, slabs. An had become s, which combined with c made x.

LOAN BURN. Burn from a grassy place. *Lean*, grassy level place.

LOANHEAD. Head of the loan. *Lean*, level grassy place. Sometimes head in a name is a corruption of *chuid*, fold.

LOCH BURN. Dark Burn. *Loch*, dark, black.

LOCHEND. Small loch. *Lochan*, diminutive of *loch*, lake, pool.

LOCHRIN. Point of the loch. *Rinn*, point; *loch*, pool, canal basin, lake.

LOCKHART HALL, for *Choill Loch Ard*. Hill of the black hill. *Choill, coill* aspirated, hill; *loch*, dark; *ard*, hill.

LOGAN LEE. Grassy place in a little howe. *Lagan*, small howe; ley (Scotch), grass-land.

LOGANBANK. Level terrace near a little howe. *Lagan*, diminutive of *lag*, howe.

LOGIE GREEN. Green place in a little howe *Logan*, diminutive of *lag*, howe. An becomes ie in Scotch.

LONG EDGE, LONG HEAD, LONG RIG, LONGBIRN, LONGERWOOD, LONGFORD, LONGHANGMAN, LONGHILL, LONG KNOWE, LONGMUIR RIG HEAD, LONGSHAW, LONGSIDE, LONGTHORN. In these names long represents *lamhan*, diminutive of *lamh*, hill, in which mha had become silent and had been lost Mh being equal to nasal v lan had become lang, which had afterwards been made long Edge is *aod*, hill, brae, with g faintly sounded after d, head is *chuid*, *cuid* aspirated, fold, c in ch being lost; rig is *ruigh*, slope, hill; birn is *bearna*, gap, er is *airidh*, shieling; hangman is *man*, hill, and *fhang*, *fang* aspirated, fold, with f lost, hill is a translation of long, knowe is *cnocan*, small hill. Longmuir Rig Head means fold on the slope of the muir on the hill, shaw is a wood, side represents *suidhe*, place, farm town; thorn is *carn* aspirated because it was supposed that it was qualified by long, believed to be an adjective

LONGFAUGH. Long field. *Fath* (Irish), field of cultivated land. Th had become gh. Long might be for *lamhan*, hill. See Long Edge

LOQUHARIOT. Loch on a shieling. *Loch*, pool, loch; *airidh*, shieling.

LOTHIAN BRIDGE, LOTHIAN BURN, LOTHIAN RIGG. Lothian is *leoidean*, diminutive of *leud*, side. Rigg is *ruigh*, slope on the side of a hill.

LOUPIELEE Bend at a grassy place. *Luban*, diminutive of *lub*, bend. An normally becomes ie.

LOVER'S LOUP, for *Lub Lamh Airidh*. Bend in the shieling hill. *Lub*, bend; *lamh*, hill; *airidh*, shieling B in *lub* has become p; mh in *lamh* has become v; idh has been lost, and s had been added to r to obtain an English possessive.

LOWHOLM, for *Lamh Tholm*. Hill. *Lamh*, hill; *tholm*, *tolm* aspirated, low round hill. Mh is sometimes equal to ou. T in *tholm* is silent and it had been lost

LOWRIES DEN. Fox's den. Lowrie is a name given in Scotland to a fox because when approaching his prey he lowers his ears on his neck. A fox is sometimes called tod-lowrie.

LUFFEN, for *Fhluich Bheinn*. Wet hill *Fhluich*, wet; *bheinn*, *beinn* aspirated, hill. Fh in *fluich* is silent, and ch had become ph, which is f. *Beinn* had been aspirated because it follows its adjective. Bh is equal to v, which has here become f.

' LUFRA COTTAGE. The meaning is obscure. It may mean cottage at a small fold. *Luth*, changed to luf, small; *rath* (th silent), fold, circle, enclosure.

LUGATE WATER. Little water. *Lughad*, littleness. The Lugate is less than the Gala.

LUGTON. Town in a hollow *Lag*, hollow.

LYDEN, for *Dein Leigead*, Den of milking. *D ir*, den; *leigeadh*, milking.

LYMPHOY, for *Lamh Chuith.* Hill of the fold. *Lamh*, hill ; *chuith, cuith* aspirated, fold.

MAGGIE BOWIES. Yellow little plain. *Maghan*, diminutive of *magh*, plain ; *buidhe*, yellow. An had been made both ie and s.

MAIDEN BRIDGE, MAIDEN HILL. Middle bridge, and Middle hill. *Meadhon*, middle.

MAINS. Farm occupied by the owner of an estate. Terrae Dominicales (Latin), lord's lands. From dominicales comes the English word domains, which in Scotland has become mains.

MAITLAND BRIDGE. Wooden bridge shod with broken stones, called metalling.

MAKIMRICH, for *Maghan Ruigh.* Little level place at the foot of a slope. *Maghan*, small plain ; *ruigh*, slope.

MALCOMSTON, for *Baile Meall Coimh-meas.* Town at a hill of common pasture. *Baile*, town ; *meall*, hill ; *coimh-meas*, common, held jointly by several persons.

MALLENY. Abounding in hillocks. *Meallanach*, abounding in knolls.

MANSFIELD. Field on a hill. *Man*, hill. S had been added because an is sometimes a plural termination.

MANSON HILL. Hill. *Man*, hill ; *sithean* (th silent), hill.

MARCH BANK. The meaning of this name cannot be given with certainty. March may mean big fold. *Mor*, big ; *chuith, cuith* aspirated, fold. Bank may originally have been *chuit, cuit* aspirated, fold, corrupted into white, and turned into Gaelic by *ban*, white, with the addition of euphonic k.

MARCH WELL, perhaps for Marsh town. Marrisch, Scotch for marsh ; *bhaile, baile* aspirated, town. *Bhaile* is pronounced waile, which would readily become well.

MARFIELD. Hill field. *Mur*, hill.

MARL LAW. Limestone hill. *Marla*, clay, marble, limestone.

MARTELLO TOWER. Tower with several stories having vaulted roofs and cannon on the top, like a tower on Cape Mortella in Corsica. Mortella (Italian), wild myrtle.

MASON'S MAINS. Mason, for *Masan*, diminutive of *mas*, beautiful ; mains, farm occupied by the owner of an estate. See Mains.

MASTER CLEUGH, MASTERTON. Master, for *Maitheas Tir.* Good land. *Maitheas* (th silent), good, goodness ; *tir*, land.

MATTHEW'S LINN. Beautiful linn. *Maitheas*, beauty ; *linne*, linn, pool, burn, waterfall.

MAULDSLIE. Bare hill. *Maol*, bald ; *sliabh* (bh silent), hill, D is a euphonic insertion.

MAURICEWOOD, perhaps Marsh wood. Marrisch (Scotch), marsh.

MAVISHALL. Place of bounty. *Maitheas*, goodness, kindness. Th had become bh equal to v.

MAYFIELD. Level field. *Magh* (gh equal to y), plain.

MAYSHADE   Level field. *Magh*, plain; shade (English), division

MEADOWHEAD. Head of a meadow, or Fold on a meadow. *Chuid*, cuid aspirated, fold. C, being silent, had been lost.

MEALOWTHER. Hill of the fold on a shieling. *Meall*, hill, *chuith*, *cuith* aspirated, fold; *airidh*, shieling. Ch in *chuith* had been lost.

MEAN BURN. Small burn *Mean*, small

MEGMILLAR, for *Meug Mill Airidh*. Great hill of the shieling. Meug, for *meud*, greatness; *mill*, variant of *meall*, hill, *airidh*, shieling. Dh, equal to y, with its antecedent vowel had been lost.

MEIKLE LAW. Big hill. Meikle (Scotch), big; *lamh*, hill.

MELVILLE. If this is a Gaelic name its original form had been *Meall Bheinn*, both parts of which mean hill. *Meall*, hill, *bheinn*, *beinn*, hill, aspirated because it seemed to qualify *meall* It had been added to *meall* to explain and expand it Bh sounds v, and nn sometimes becomes ll.

MELVIN HALL. Mansion at a hill. *Meall*, hill, *bheinn*, *beinn* aspirated, hill. The second part had been added to explain the first. Melvin may be a personal name.

MERCHIESTON, for *Baile Mor Chos*. Town at the big fold. *Baile*, town, *mor*, big, *chos*, *cos* aspirated, fold. *Cos* is aspirated because it follows its adjective.

MESTON, MISTON, for *Baile Maise* Town of beauty *Baile*. town, *maise*, beauty.

MID RIG. Middle Slope. *Ruigh*, slope of a hill.

MIDDLE HEAD. Middle fold. *Chuid*, *cuid* aspirated, fold C in ch is silent

MILLER'S MOSS. Moss of the hill of the shieling. *Meall*, hill; *airidh*, shieling. Idh had been lost.

MILLHEAD. Fold on a hill. *Meall*, hill, *chuid*, *cuid* aspirated, fold. C silent had been lost

MILLHILL Hill. *Meall*, hill. The second part is a translation of the first

MOAT. Seat of a barony court. *Mod*, court of justice.

MONKS RIG. Slope of a hill belonging to a convent. *Ruigh*, hill slope.

MONTEITH. Warm moor. *Monadh*, moor, *teith* (Irish), warm, smooth.

MONTMARLE Hill of limestone. *Monadh*, hill, *murla*, clay, marl, limestone Marle might represent the Scotch word marled, having spots of various colours mixed together.

MONTROSE. Hill at a point. *Monadh*, hill; *ros*, point

MOORFOOT. Moor of the fold. *Chuit*, *cuit* aspirated, fold. Ch became ph, equal to f

MOREDUN, MORTON. Big hill. *Mor*, big, *dun*, hill.

MOUNT LOTHIAN. Small place on the side of a hill *Monadh*, hill, *levidean*, diminutive of *lei d*, side, formed from *l* · · l form of *leud*.

MOUNT MAIN. Both parts mean hill. *Monadh* hill; *man*, hill.

MUILEPUTCHIE, for *Muil Chuit Chuith.* Hill of the fold. *Muil,* a variant of *maoile,* bare hill ; *chuit, cuit* aspirated, fold ; *chuith, cuith* aspirated, fold.   Ch became ph, and by loss of the aspirate ph became p.   Final th is silent and had been lost.   Thus was produced muil-puit-chui, now muileputchie.   *Chuith* had been a late addition made to explain puit.

MUIRHOUSE.   House on a muir.   But house sometimes represents *chuith, cuith* aspirated, fold, and the name might mean muir of the fold.

MUIRIESTON.   Town on a small hill.   *Baile,* town, translated ; *murean,* diminutive of *mur,* hill.   Ean had become ie.

MULDRON.   Ridge of a hill.   *Meall,* hill ; *dronn,* ridge.

MUMPOT LAW. Hill of the moss-pot *Lamh,* hill; *moine,* moor ; *poit,* pot.   N becomes m before p.

MUNGO'S BRIDGE.   Bridge at the moor of the little fold. *Moine,* moor ; *cuithan,* little fold.   Th being silent had been lost, c had become g, and an had become s.

MURRAY BURN, MURRAY'S BURN, MURRAY'S POOL.   Murray and Murray's represent *Abh Mur.*   Burn of the hill.   *Abh,* burn ; *mur,* hill.   The order of the parts had been changed, and s had been added to obtain an English possessive.

MUSSELBURGH, for *Mas Coill Bruch*   Round hill.   *Mas* or *mus,* round; *coill,* hill; *bruch,* hill.   Mussel was formerly spelled muscle.

MUTTON HOLE, for *Meadhonach Choill.*   Middle hill.   *Meadhonach,* middle ; *choill, coill* aspirated, hill.   Ach became silent and was lost.   C in *choill* was lost, being silent.

NETTLINGFLAT.   Meeting-place at a plain near a burn.   *Flath* (Irish), meeting , *lian,* plain ; *net,* burn.

NEW.   New in names may be three things (1.) The English word new.   (2.) *Naomh* (pronounced nuv or new), sacred, belonging to a church or a convent.   (3.) *An Chuith,* the fold.   *An,* the ; *chuith, cuith* aspirated, fold.   *An* would lose a, *chuith* would lose ch and th, and n and ui combined would form new.

NEWBATTLE, NEWHALL, NEWHOUSE, NEWLANDRIG.   See New for the first part of the names.   Battle is for *Beathach Tulach,* birch-hill (*beathach,* birch-growing ; *tulach,* hill).   Hall is *Choill, coill* aspirated, hill.   House is *Chuith, cuith* aspirated, fold. Landrig is *Lamhan Ruigh,* slope of the hill (*lamhan,* hill ; *ruigh,* slope).   *Beathach* and *tulach* lost their aspirated letters ; *choill* lost c ; *chuith* lost c, and th became sh, from which h was lost, and huis became house ; *lamhan* lost mh, and d was added to n ; *ruigh* lost h and became rig.

NIDDRY.   Burn of the slope of a hill.   *Nid,* burn ; *ruigh,* slope at the base of a hill.

NINE SPRINGS.   Springs giving water good for washing. *Nigheachan,* washing.   Gh and ch with the intermediate vowels had been silent and had been lost   Nian, which is left, resembles in sound both *nigh an* (gh silent) maiden, and the English word nine.   Hence arose mistakes regarding the meaning of *nigheachan*. Maiden Well might mean well with soft water useful for washing clothes

NIVEN'S KNOWE Knoll of the small fold *Cnocan*, knoll, *na*, of the, *chuithan*, *cuithan* aspirated, little fold. *Na chuithan* became nivan by loss of a in *na* and chu in *chuithan*, and the change of the th to bh, which is equal to v. S was added to nivan because it ended in an, wrongly supposed to be a plural termination Nivans is now niven's.

NORTH GYLE. North fold The original form of Gyle may have been *Chuit*, *cuit* aspirated, fold. *Chuit* had been corrupted into white, which had afterwards been turned into *geal*, white, now become gyle.

NORTON. North town. Norton is north from Ratho.

OATSLEE. Grass-land at a small fold. *Chuitan*, *cuitan* aspirated, small fold, ley (Scotch), grassy place Ch had become silent and had been lost. An had wrongly been made s instead of ie. Uits had lapsed into oats.

ORCHARDFIELD. Field in which there was a pigsty on a height *Urc*, sty; *ard*, height. The name may, however, be modern.

ORMISTON, for *Oir Baile Maise*. East beautiful town. *Oir*, east, *baile* (translated), town, *maise*, beauty.

ORMSCLEUGH Cleugh on the edge of good land. *Or*, border, *maitheas* (pronounced mae-as), goodness

OTTER BURN. Broad burn. *Oth*, broad, *our*, water.

OUTERSHILL, OUTERSTON. Fold on a small piece of land. *Chuit*, *cuit* aspirated, fold, *tirean*, small piece of ground C silent was lost, and ean became s instead of ie.

OUTTER HILL. Land at the fold on a hill. Outter is for *Tir Chuit*. Land at a fold. *Tir*, land, *chuit*, *cuit* aspirated, fold.

OVER SHIELS. Upper huts. *Sealan*, plural of *seal*, shiel, hut on summer pasture.

OXENFORD. Old ford. *Aosda*, ancient Most fords had to be crossed by waggons drawn by oxen, and hence the name Oxenford would not have been distinctive.

OXENFORD MAINS. Oxen represents *Aosda*, old, ancient See Mains.

OXGANGS. Old fold. *Aosda*, ancient, *fhangan*, *fangan* aspirated, small fold *Fangan* had been aspirated because it followed its adjective. Fh had become gh, and an had been made s instead of ie.

PADDIEHALL, for *Choill Paitean*. Hill of the little hump. *Choill*, *coill* aspirated, hill; *paitean*, diminutive of *pait*, hump.

PADDY'S RIVER. River flowing from a small hump on a hill. *Paitean*, small hump. Ean had been regarded as a diminutive termination and had been made y, and also as a plural termination and had been made s.

PARADYKES, PARDIVAN, PARDOVAN, PARDUVINE, PARSON'S GREEN, PARSON-POOL, PEARIE LAW P in these names represents *chop*, *op* aspirated, hill, with cho omitted The second part is

D

airidh, shieling, summer pasture; dykes is *dubh*, black; divan and dovan are *dubh abhainn*, black stream; duvine is *dubh bheinn*, black hill, sons is *suthean*, hill, with s added because it ends in an; pool is *poll*, burn; and law is *lamh*, hill.

PATE'S HILL, PATIE'S HILL. Hill with a small hump. *Paitean*, diminutive of *pait*, hump. Ean had been regarded as a diminutive termination and made e and ie, and also as a plural termination and made s.

PATH-HEAD. Birch-wood at a fold. *Beath*, birch-wood; *chuid*, *cuid* aspirated, fold. C had been lost, being silent.

PEASEFLAT, for *Piosan Reidh*. Small flat piece of ground. *Piosan*, small piece; *reidh*, flat, level. An had become ie, afterwards made e.

PEASTON. Small town. *Pios,* small.

PEAT LAW. Peat hill. *Lamh*, hill. Mh is silent.

PEATRIG HILL. Hill with peat-moss on the slope. *Ruigh*, slope.

PEFFERMILL. Mill at the fold on the shieling. *Chuith, cuith* aspirated, fold; *airidh*, shieling. Ch had become ph, which had afterwards lost h. Th had become ph, which is equal to f. Idh of *airidh* had become silent and had been lost.

PEGGY'S LEA, PEGGY'S MILL. Peggy's represents *Picean*, small pointed hill. Ean had been made y as a diminutive termination, and s as a plural.

PENDREICH. Hill of the hawthorn. *Fin*, hill; *draigh*, hawthorn. F is equal to ph, and h having been lost pin was left, now made pen.

PENICUIK, for *Beinn a' Cnuic*. Hill of the hill. *Beinn*, hill; *a'*, of the; *cnuic*, genitive of *cnoc*, hill. N had become silent and had been lost.

PENNYWELL. Well supposed to have medicinal virtues. It had been visited by sick and infirm persons, who drank of the well or washed sores with its water and then dropped coins into it. These might formerly have been given to a priest for services rendered at the well on certain days.

PENNYWHIGAM BURN, for *Beinn na h-Uigean* Burn. Burn of the hill with a little nook. *Beinn*, hill; *na*, of the; *h* euphonic; *uigean*, diminutive of *uig*, curve, bend.

PENTLAND. Hill. *Beinn*, hill; *lamhan*, hill. Euphonic t had been added to *beinn*, and euphonic d to *lamhan*.

PENTLAND HILLS. Hills. *Beinnte*, plural of *beinn*, hill, *lamhan*, plural of *lamh*, hill. Final e in *beinnte* had been lost. Mh in *lamhan* had been lost, and euphonic d had been added to n. In Irish several nouns have tean in the plural, which may be shortened to te. *Baile* has both *bailtean* and *bailte* in the plural.

PIERSHILL, for *Peirse Coill*. Row of houses at a hill. *Peirse*, row; *coill*, hill.

PIGSKNOWES. Little pointed knoll. *Picean*, diminutive of *pic*, pointed hill; *cnocan*, diminutive of *cnoc*, hill.

PILLAR KNOWE. Knoll on a shieling on which there was a fort or a shelter   *Cnocan*, little hill ; *pill*, genitive form of *peall*, fort, sheltered place , *airidh*, shieling.   Idh had been lost.

PILMUIR, for *Moine Puill*. Moor of the pool.   *Moine*, moor ; *puill*, genitive of *poll*, pool, burn.

PILRIG. Fold on a hillside.   *Peall*, protected place, peel , *ruigh*, slope at the base of a hill.   Large peels were enclosed with stone walls ; small with trunks of trees planted in the ground, to which skins and mats were attached to give shelter

PILTON. Town at a peel. See Pilrig.

PINKIE. Fold   The original form of the name had been *Chuitail, cuitail* aspirated, fold, which had been corrupted into whitehill. This had been turned again into Gaelic by *fincan*, white hill (*fin*, hill ; *can*, white). F is equal to ph, which by the loss of the aspirate became p   An was erroneously supposed to be a diminutive termination and was changed to ie. Pincie became pinkie.

PIRN KNOWE. Knoll with a gap in it.   *Bearna*, gap.

PIRNIEFIELD, for *Achadh Bearna*   Place where there is a gap or long howe. *Achadh*, field, place ; *bearua*, gap, gorge, trench.

PIRNTATON   Burn of the valley of delights   *Bearna*, valley, gap ; *tartean*, plural of *tarte*, pleasure.

PLAY HILL. Hill of milking   *Bleoghann*, milking. Ann became ie, which was lost, and gh is equal to y.

PLAYWELL   Well at a milking fold   *Bleoghann*, milking   Gh is equal to y, and ann became ie and was lost.

PLEA KNOWE. Knoll of milking.   *Bleoghann*, milking. Gh had become silent and had been lost. Ann had became ie and had been lost.

PIENPLOTH, for *Pliadhan Plod*. Small bit of ground at a pool. *Pliadhan* (dh silent), diminutive of *pliad*, piece of ground ; *plod*, pool

PLOWLAND HILL. Hill where cows were milked. *Bleoghann*, milking , *lamhan*, little hill

PODLIE STONE. Podlie is one of the names for young coal fish, and these may have been caught at this stone at full tide.

POGBIE, for *Bog Bith*   Quiet moist place. *Bog*, wet ground ; *bith*, quiet

POLBETH. Burn of birches   *Poll*, pool, burn ; *bith*, birch.

POLTON. Pool town   *Poll*, pool, burn.

POMATHORN, for *Poll a' Charn*   Burn from the hill. *Poll*, burn , *a'*, of the , *charn*, carn aspirated, hill.

POT LAW, for *Lamh Poit*. Hill of the pool. *Lamh*, hill ; *poit*, pot, pool.

POWFASTLE   Burn of the castle   *Poll*, burn , *chaisteal*, *caisteal* aspirated, fort. Ch had become ph, which is f.

POWIES PATH   Foot road near a small river. *Pollan*, small burn. An had been made ie by some and s by others, improperly, and both had been added to pow, a soft form of *poll*, burn.

PRESTON. Town at a bush. *Preas*, bush.

PRESTONHALL. Preston, for *Baile Preas*. Town at a bushy place. *Baile*, town ; *preas*, bush.

PRESTONHOLM. Bushy place at a town on a riverside haugh. *Preas*, bush ; holm (English), flat land near a river.

PRIEST'S BOG. Moist place where bushes grow. *Bog*, soft moist ground ; *preas*, bush

PRINGLE HILL. Pringle is Hoppringle with hop lost. See Hoppringle.

PUMPHERSTON, for *Baile Pund-fhear*. Town of the pundler. *Baile*, town , *pund-fhear*, pundler, officer who impounded straying cattle. S converted *fhear* into an English possessive.

QUARREL BURN. Quarry burn. *Coireall*, quarry.

RADICAL ROAD. Road on the side of a hill. *Ruigh*, slope ; *a'*, of the ; *choill, coill* aspirated, hill Radical Road is near the base of Arthur's Seat.

RAESHAW Wood at a fold. *Rath* (th silent), fold ; shaw (English), wood.

RAMSLACK, perhaps for *Riamhach Lamh* Grey hill. *Riamhach*, a variant of *riabhach*, grey ; *lamh*, hill. The sound of mh is almost the same as that of bh.

RANSFIELD, for *Achadh Rathan*. Field of the small stone circle *Achadh*, field ; *rathan* (th silent), diminutive of *rath*, circle, fold, fank S is an insertion made to obtain an English possessive.

RASHIEHILL. Slope at the base of a hill. *Ruighean*, diminutive of *ruigh*, shieling, slope of a hill where cultivation begins.

RATHO. Small fold *Rathan*, diminutive of *rath*, circle, fold. An had become ie, which had been changed to o

RATHO BYRES, for *Bathach Ratha*. Byres at a fold *Bathach*, byre, cow-house ; *ratha*, genitive of *rath*, fold, circle, row of stone pillars round a grave.

RAVEL SYKE. Drain from a fold on a hill. *Rath*, fold ; *aill*, hill. Th had become bh, equal to v.

RAVELEIG, for *Rath Ruigh Aill*. Fold on the slope of a hill. *Rath*, fold, circle ; *ruigh*, slope ; *aill*, hill. Th had become bh, equal to v. *Ruigh* and *aill* had been transposed to avoid a hiatus.

RAVELSTON. Town on the side of a hill. *Ruigh*, slope near the base of a hill ; *aill*, hill.

RAVENS CLEUGH, RAVENS ROCK, RAVENSHAUGH, RAVENSNOOK. Ravens is for *Ruigh Bheinn*. Slope on a hill. *Ruigh*, slope at the base of a hill , *bheinn, beinn* aspirated, hill. S had been inserted to make raven possessive. In some places *ruigh bheinn* has become ruthven.

RAW CAMP. Ancient fold, supposed to be a Roman camp. *Rath* (th silent), fold, circle round a grave.

RAWBURN, RAWBURN HEAD. Burn at a fold. *Rath* (th silent), fold. Head is *chuid*, *cuid* aspirated, fold C, being silent, had been lost.

REDFORD, REDSIDE. Level ford, level place. *Reidh*, level, *suidhe*, place.

REDHEUGHS. Steep red banks. *Heugh* (Scotch), steep bank without vegetation.

REMOTE. Plain of assembly. *Reidh*, plain, *mod*, assembly.

RESTALRIG, for *Rust Ruigh Aill*. *Rust* means hill It had been added to explain the original name. *Ruigh Aill* means slope of the hill *Ruigh*, slope; *aill*, hill. It is said that an old form of the name was Lestalrig, which would have represented *Lios Ruigh Aill*, fold of the slope of the hill. *Lios*, fold, *ruigh*, slope at the base of a hill, *aill*, hill.

RHYND LODGE. Lodge at a point. *Rinn*, point D is a euphonic addition to n. Rhynd may be a personal name.

RICCARTON, for *Baile Ruigh Ard*. Town on the slope of a hill *Baile* (translated), town, *ruigh*, slope; *ard*, height.

RISLAND. Muir on a hill *Riasg*, wet moor *lamhan*, little hill. D is a euphonic addition to n

ROADS, for *Ruighean* Slight slope. *Ruighean*, diminutive of *ruigh*, slope at the base of a hill Gh and dh are pronounced in the same way, hence g and d are confounded An had improperly been made s instead of ie.

ROBIN'S WELL Well in a bushy place. *Roibeach*, bushy, shaggy

RODDINGLAW, for *Ruadhan Lamh* Little red place on a hill. *Ruadhan*, diminutive of *ruadh*, red, *lamh* (mh silent), hill.

ROMAN CAMP The place called by this name is an old fold

ROSE CLEUGH, ROSE VIEW, ROSEBERY, ROSEBURN, ROSEHILL, ROSEMAINS, ROSEMAY, ROSLIN. Rose and ros represent *ros*, point. Rose Cleugh means steep bank at a point, Rose View, point from which a view is seen, Rosebery is *ros*, point, and *biorach*, pointed, Roseburn is a point between two burns, Rosehill, hill with a point; Rosemains, farm at a point, Rosemay, point of a hill projecting into a plain—*magh*, plain, Roslin, waterfall at a point of land—*linne*, linn, fall

ROSE WELL, for *Bhaile Ros* Town on a point of land *Bhaile*, baile aspirated, town, *ros*, point *Baile* had been aspirated and put last Bh is equal to w, and *bhaile* had been pronounced waile and, when final e had been lost, well.

ROTTENROW, for *Rath Rotan* Circle on a round little hill *Rath* (pronounced raw), stone circle, fold, *rotan*, round little hill.

ROUTING HILL. Slope of a hill. *Ruighean*, diminutive of *ruigh*, slope, shieling.

ROUTING WELL, for *Baile Ruighean*. Town on a hillside *Baile*, town, *ruighean*, diminutive of *ruigh*, slope of a hill *Baile*, made *bhaile* and corrupted into well, had been transferred to the end.

ROW, ... law (Scot) ... ...

Rowater, for *Ruigh Uachdar*. Upper slope. *Ruigh* (gh silent), slope, shieling ; *uachdar* (ch silent), upper.

Royston. Small hill. *Rustan*, small hill.

Rullion Green, for *Ruigh Ailean*. Green plain on a slope. *Ruigh*, slope of a hill, shieling ; *ailean*, green

Rusha. Slope of a hill. *Ruighe*. Slope at the base of a hill.

Ruther Law, for *Lamh Ruigh Airidh*. Hill of the slope of the shieling. *Lamh*, hill ; *ruigh*, slope ; *airidh*, shieling. Mh is equal to w ; gh became th ; and idh, being silent, had been lost.

Saint Ann's, for *Sithean Innis*. Hill at a fold. *Sithean* (th silent), hill , *innis*, fold, enclosure. Euphonic t had been added to final n. *Innis* has frequently become Ann's and Annie's.

Saint Bernard's. If this name is of Gaelic origin it repre-sents *Sithean Bearn Ardan*. Gap in a little hill. *Sithean*, little hill , *bearn*, gap ; *ardan*, little hill. *Sithean* had lost th with the flanking vowels ; and an of *ardan* had become s instead of ie. Euphonic t had been added to *sithean*. The last part had been added to explain the first after it had been corrupted.

Saint Leonards. If this name is of Gaelic origin it is a corruption of *Sithean Lean Ardan*. Hillock of the level plain. *Sithean* (th silent), small hill ; *lean*, plain ; *ardan*, small hill. Euphonic t had been added to *sithean*, and an of *ardan* had improperly been changed to s, instead of ie.

Salisbury Craigs, for *Creagan Sealan Bruch*. Cliffs at the shieling on the hill. *Creagan*, plural of *creag*, cliff, rock ; *sealan*, shieling, summer pasture , *bruch*, hill   An of *creagan* normally became s, being plural, but *sealan* is not plural and it was a mistake to change an into is   Arthur's Seat had anciently been common summer pasture for the cows of the burgesses, which had been herded by men paid jointly by the owners.

Salterford, for *Ath Tir Sath*. Ford at the land of the cattle. *Ath*, ford ; *tir*, land ; *sath*, drove, herd. Th is silent and had been lost, but a being long l had been inserted, as in calm.

Salters Road. Road for cattle going to and from a shieling. *Sath* (Irish), drove, cattle ; *airidh*, shieling. L is frequently inserted after a where it ought not to be, and sometimes it is omitted where it ought to be. S is an insertion made to make salter possessive.

Saltersyke, Small drain from the land of the shieling Syke (Scotch), small stream from a wet place ; *seal*, shieling ; *tir*, land.

Salvandi. Black little field. *Sealbhan*, little field for cattle , *dubh*, black. Bh is equal to v, but it may be silent.

Sauchan Side. Small pleasant place. *Samhachan*, diminu-tive of *samhach*, quiet, pleasant ; *suidhe*, place. Mh, being silent, had been dropped.

Saughland. Pleasant hill. *Samhach*, pleasant ; *lamhan*, little hill. Euphonic d had been added to n.

SAUGHLY, perhaps for *Samhach Lamh.* Peaceful hill. *Samhach,* peaceful, quiet; *lamh* (mh silent), hill.

SAUGHS, for *Samhachan.* Quiet little place. *Samhachan,* diminutive of *samhach,* quiet, pleasant. Mh is silent and had been lost. An had wrongly been made s instead of ie.

SAUGHTON Pleasant place. *Samhach* (mh equal to u), mild, pleasant.

SCADLAW, SCALD LAW. Hill where cattle were received to pasture on payment of a money rent. Sgat (Norse), rent; *lamh,* hill.

SCARCE RIG. Rocky slope. *Sgeireach,* rocky; *ruigh,* slope.

SCREW WOOD. Wood on rocky ground. *Sgreig* (Irish), rocky ground. Screw might represent *sgreuchagach,* abounding in jackdaws.

SCROGGY HILL. Hill growing stunted worthless trees and bushes *Sgrogag,* stunted timber.

SCROOF HILL Hill whose surface had been taken away for fuel. *Sgriob,* to make bare. Or, Hill of bad pasture. *Sgriobhach* (Irish), affording bad pasture. Or, Dry hill. *Sgreubh,* to dry up.

SELL MOOR Moor of the shiel *Seal,* shiel, temporary residence on hill pasture.

SELMS, for *Sealbhan.* Small herd of cattle. *Sealbhan,* diminutive of *sealbh,* herd of cattle. Bh became mh, both sounded v; and an was improperly made s instead of ie. Sealmhs lapsed into selms.

SERGEANTS LAW. Dry hill. *Searganach,* dry; *lamh,* hill.

SHANK HILL. *Sithean,* hill. S before i is equal to sh Th is silent, and euphonic k had been added to n

SHAW BURN. Burn of the bushy place. Shaw, grove, small wood.

SHAWFAIR. Wooded hill. Shaw (Scotch), wooded, *fair,* hill.

SHEAR BURN. Black burn. *Sear,* dark, black. S before e sounds sh

SHEARER KNOW, for *Cnapan Sear Airidh.* Knoll of the black shiel. *Cnapan,* knoll, *sear,* black, *airidh,* shiel. The shiels were residences for women in charge of cows on hill pasture. They were built of black mossy sods

SHEARS, for *Searan.* Little black place. *Searan,* diminutive of *sear* (Irish), black.

SHEELING HILL. Hill to which cattle were sent in summer to be away from growing crops. Previous to 1750 fields were not fenced, and all the arable land on farms was under crop every year. *Sealan,* shieling.

SHEIL BURN. Burn passing a hut on a shieling. *Seal,* shiel, temporary residence on summer pasture.

SHEIL KNOWE. Knoll on which there were huts for persons in charge of cattle on summer pasture

SHERIFFHALL, for *Coill Sear Abh.* Hill of the black water *Coill,* hill; *sear,* dark; *abh,* water. *Coill* had been made *choill*

and put last, then c being silent had been lost, and oi had been
made a to obtain an English word Bh had become ph, which
is f.

SHEWINGTON. Hill town. *Sithean* (pronounced shean), hill.
Th had become bh, which is equal to w, and an became ing.

SHIEL. Temporary summer residence for persons in charge
of cattle on hill pasture. *Seal*, hut, residence far away from
cultivated land.

SHINBANES. Fold. Originally *Chuitail*, *cuitail* aspirated,
fold, which had been corrupted into whitehill. This had been
turned into Gaelic by *sitheanban*, white hill (*sithean*, hill ; *ban*,
white). *Sithean* is pronounced shean. An of *ban* was improperly made es, which was added to *ban*, and shean banes is
now shinbanes.

SHIRE HAUGH. Black haugh. *Sear*, black. S before e is
equal to sh.

SHOESTANES. Hill. The oldest part of the name is the last,
which had been *sithean*, hill, to which had been added s because
it ended in an, erroneously supposed to be a plural termination.
By dropping i and h steans was produced, now made stanes.
Then had been prefixed *sith*, hill, pronounced she, but now
made shoe.

SHOTHEAD. Field of the fold. Shot (English), separate field,
small farm ; *chuid*, *cuid* aspirated, fold.

SIDE. Place. *Suidhe*, place.

SILVER HAUGH. Haugh on a shieling for cattle. *Sealbh*,
cattle ; *airidh*, shieling.

SILVERBURN. Burn of the shieling for cattle. *Sealbh*, cattle ;
airidh, shieling.

SILVERKNOWES for *Cnapan Sealbhar*. Knoll of the herd of
cattle. *Cnapan*, knoll ; *sealbhar*, herd of cattle An had been
supposed to be a plural termination and had been translated
by es.

SINKIE, for *Sithean Cuith*. Hill of the fold. *Sithean*
(contracted to sin), hill ; *cuith* (th silent), fold. Sin cui became
sinkie.

SISTER'S HOLE, for *Seis Tirean Choill*. Pleasant little place
on a hill. *Seis*, pleasant ; *tirean*, diminutive of *tir*, land ;
choill, *coill* aspirated, hill C, being silent, had been lost.

SIT BURN. Hill burn. *Sith*, hill.

SKELTIE MUIR. Extensive moor. *Sgaoilte*, spread out.

SKIVO Beautiful place. *Sgiamhach*, beautiful. Mh is
equal to v. Skibo is the same as Skivo, but mh had become
bh.

SKOTIE BURN. *Skotie* represents *Eas Cuitan*. Burn of the
little ford. *Eas*, burn ; *cuitan*, little fold. Ea of *eas* had been
lost, and an of *cuitan* had become ie.

SLATEBARNS. Gap in a hill. *Sliobh*, hill ; *bearnas*, gap.

SLATEFORD. Ford protected against erosion by stems of es
laid up and down in the bottom. *Slat*, rod.

SLATEHEUGH. Steep bank on a hill *Sliabh*, hill The name may mean slate quarry.

SLATY ROW. Row of houses on the hills. *Sleibhte*, plural of *sliabh*, hill.

SLAUGHTER HOUSE House on hill land. *Sliabh*, hill, *tir*, land.

SMEATON. Small place. *Smiotan*, diminutive of *smiot*, small portion.

SNYPE, for *Eas na Peic.* Burn of the long strip. *Eas*, burn, *na*, of the, *peic* (Irish), long tail The sound of ea had been lost, a became y, and final c had been aspirated and had subsequently been lost. There is a long narrow strip of land at Snype between a burn and a road.

SOLE. Wet place. *Soghail* (gh silent), wet.

SOUTRA. The first part of the name is accented and it had originally been last. Perhaps for *Rath Suth.* Fold where cows were milked *Rath*, fold, circle, *suth* (Early Irish), milk.

SOW. Wet place. *Sugh*, wet.

SOWBURNRIG. Burn of the wet slope *Sugh*, wetness; *ruigh*, slope on a hill.

SOWRIG BURN. Burn from a wet hill slope. *Sugh*, moisture; *ruigh*, slope of a hill.

SPITTAL. Hospital. Hospitalia (Latin), apartments for strangers.

SPREAD Place for cattle. *Spreidh*, cattle.

SPREADS. Small place for cattle. *Spreidhean*, diminutive of *spreidh*, cattle. Ean had improperly been made s.

STAGEBANK. Steep bank. Stage is the English word staid sounded as if d were followed by ye. In Gaelic dh and gh both sound y.

STAGEHALL. Upstanding hill Stage is the English word staid, standing up, with the sound of ye added to d. Hall is *choill*, *coill* aspirated, hill C in ch is silent and had been lost.

STAIR ARMS. Inn with a sign showing the shield and coat of arms of the Earls of Stair.

STANDING STONES Circle of stone pillars guarding a prehistoric British grave. In the centre of the circle there was a small chamber or an urn containing incinerated bones.

STEEL PARK Park of the spring *Steal*, gushing spring

STELL KNOWE. Knoll where there is a shelter for sheep

STILL BRIDGE. Bridge over a rushing burn *Steall*, gushing spring In England *steall* sometimes means stagnant water in a ditch.

STIRLING. Cliff of a hill. *Stor*, cliff; *lamhan*, diminutive of *lamh*, hill. Mh being silent had been lost, but being equal to nasal v it has caused g to be added to final n

STOBBIN DEAN. Den on a small sharp-pointed hill *Dean*, den, *stoban*, diminutive of *stob*, pointed hill

STOBGREEN. (hass) ... ... sing to a point.

STOBHILL. Pointed hill. *Stob*, point of a hill.

STOBS. Little pointed hill. *Stoban*, diminutive of *stob*, pointed hill. An became s instead of ie.

STOCKBRIDGE. Bridge formed of a solid piece of wood. *Stoc*, trunk of a tree, solid wood.

STOTFIELD. Field for bullocks. Stot (English), steer, bullock.

STOW. Pointed hill. *Stobh, stob* with b aspirated, pointed hill. Bh is sounded as ou.

STRAITON. Little lane. *Sraidean*, diminutive of *sraid*, lane, street.

STRUTHER. Stream. *Sruthair* (Irish), stream.

SUMMER KNOWE. Wet knoll. *Sughmhor*, wet. Gh is silent, and h in mhor serves to show that m is nasal, but it is not sounded itself.

SUMMERSIDE. Wet place. *Sughmhor*, wet; *suidhe*, place. Gh is silent, and h in mhor is also silent but it makes m nasal.

SUNBURY. Both parts of the name mean hill. *Sithean* (th silent), hill; *bruch*, hill.

SWALLOW LAW. Conspicuous hill. *Sualach*, conspicuous, famous; *lamh*, hill.

SWANSTON Town in a wet place. *Sughan* (gh silent), wetness.

SWAREHOUSE for *Sughar Chuith*. Wet fold. *Sughar*, wet; *chuith, cuith*, aspirated, fold. Gh is equal to y, c in ch is silent, and th had become sh but had afterwards lost the aspirate h. This produced suyarhuis, now made swarehouse.

SWEETHOPE, for *Suidhe Chop*. Place on a hill. *Suidhe*, place; *chop, cop* aspirated, hill, hill-top. C silent had been lost.

SWINE'S CLEUGH. Wet cliff. *Sughan*, wetness; *cleugh*, steep bank. Gh is equal to y. An had been made s in the belief that it was a plural termination.

SYMINGTON. Town in a little quiet place. *Baile* translated, town; *seimhean*, diminutive of *seimhe*, mildness, quietness.

TARTAN HILL. Hillock. *Tartan* (Irish), hillock.

TATHIE KNOWE. Knoll frequently visited. *Tathaich*, resort.

TEMPLE. Land belonging to the Knights Templars of Jerusalem.

TEMPLE HILL. *Choill, coill*, aspirated, hill. C is silent in ch.

TEMPLE HOUSE. House which had belonged to the Knights Templars.

TENANTSMARCH. Marsh of the mall burn. *Tainan*, diminutive of *tain* (Irish), water.

THICKSIDE RIG, for *Ruigh Suidhe Tigh*. Slope on which there is the site of a house. *Ruigh*, slope; *suidhe*, site; *tigh*, house. In Irish *tigh* as an adjective means thick.

THORNTON, for *Baile Charn*. Town on a hill. *Baile*, town; *charn, carn* aspirated, hill. Ch had become th.

THORNYCROOK, for *Charnach Cnoc*. Stony hill. *Charnach, carnach* aspirated, stony; *cnoc* (pronounced croc), hill. The original form of the name must have been *Carnach Chnoc*, because the adjective precedes its noun.

THRASHIE HILL. Heathery Hill. *Fraochach*, heathery. F is equal to ph, which had become th, and ch had become sh. Ach had become ie.

THRASHIEDEAN Heathery den. *Fraochach*, heathery, *dein*, den. See Thrashie Hill.

THREIPMUIR Muir of the hill. *Triath*, hill.

TIPPER WELL. Well. *Tobar*, well.

TIPPERLINN. Well at a waterfall. *Tobar*, well, *linne*, waterfall.

TODDLE BURN. Fox-hole burn. Tod (Scotch), fox

TODHOLE KNOWE. Knoll where there was a fox's hole In some places there are ancient sea beaches, in which foxes made long holes, narrow at the mouth but wide inside.

TOD'S CAIRN Heap of stones frequented for shelter by foxes.

TOR. Steep hill *Torr*, steep, flat-topped hill

TORCRAIK. Both parts mean hill. *Torr*, steep hill, *creach*, hill.

TORDUFF Black hill *Torr*, steep abrupt hill, *dubh*, black.

TORFICHEN HILL. Hill of the little fold *Torr*, steep, abrupt hill, *chuithan, cuithan* aspirated, small fold. Ch became ph or f, and th became ch.

TORGEITH. Windy hill. *Torr*, steep, abrupt hill; *gaothach*, windy.

TORMAIN. Both parts of the name mean hill. *Torr*, steep, abrupt hill; *man*, hill

TORMYWHEEL. Hill of the fold. *Torr*, steep hill, *na*, of the; *chuithail* (th silent), *cuithail* aspirated, fold

TORPHIN HILL. The three parts of the name all mean hill *Torr*, steep, abrupt hill; *fin*, hill Ph is equal to f

TORSONCE. Hill of prosperity. *Torr*, hill; *sonas*, good fortune.

TORWEAVING. Hill of the little fold *Torr*, steep abrupt hill; *chuithan, cuithan* aspirated, little fold Ch became bh, equal to w; th became bh, equal to v; and an became ing

TOWN LAW, for *Dun Lamh.* Hill. *Dun*, hill, *lamh*, hill.

TOWNHEAD Hill of the fold. *Dun*, hill, *chuid, cuid* aspirated, fold.

TOXSIDE, for *Suidhe Tulach.* Place on a hill. *Suidhe*, place, *tulach*, hill. Toxside might mean hillside.

TRINITY. Church dedicated to the Holy Trinity. *Trinitas* (Latin), three in one.

TROQUHAN Originally *Chuitail, cuitail* aspirated, fold, corrupted into whitehill, which had again been turned into Gaelic by *triathcan*, white hill (*triath*, hill, *can*, white). Th in *triath* had been lost because silent, but it aspirated c in *can*, making it *chan*, now quhan

TROWS. Cultivated land *Treobharhas*, farm of arable land. The aspirated letters with their vowels would readily become silent and be lost.

TURNHOUSE HILL. Hill of the fold. *Torr*, steep hill; *na*, of the; *chuith, cuith* aspirated, fold. C in ch is silent, and huith had become house.

TURNIEDYKES, for *Torr an Dubhan*. Black hill. *Torr*, steep hill, *an*, of the; *dubhan*, blackness. An had become s instead of ie.

TURNIEMOON, for *Torr na Moine*. Hill of the moor. *Torr*, flat-topped hill; *na*, of the; *moine*, moor.

TYNE. River. *Tain* (Irish), water.

UNTHANK. The fold. *An*, the; *fhang, fang* aspirated, fold, fank. Fh had become th, and k had been added to g for euphony.

VAULAND BURN. Burn of the big hill. Vauland, for *Lamhan Bhagh*. Hill of bigness. *Lamhan* (mh silent), diminutive of *lamh*, hill, with euphonic d added; *bhagh, bagh* aspirated, bulk, size. Bh is equal to v.

VEIN. Hill. *Bheinn, beinn* aspirated, hill.

VENTURE FAIR. Hill of the fold. Originally Venture had been *Chuitail, cuitail* aspirated, fold, which had been corrupted into whitehill. This had been turned into Gaelic by *bhantorr*, white hill (*bhan, ban* aspirated, white, *torr*, hill), and *bhantorr* became venture. *Fair*, hill, is a late addition made to explain ture for *torr*

VERTER, for *Tir Bhior*. Land of the well. *Tir*, land, *bhior*, *bior* aspirated, well. Bh is equal to v.

VOGRIE, for *Ruigh Bheag*. Small shieling. *Ruigh*, slope of a hill, shieling; *bheag*, feminine of *beag*, small. Bh is sounded v.

WADEINBURN, for *Braon Bhadain*. Burn of the little bushy place. *Braon*, hill burn; *bhadain*, genitive aspirated of *badan*, little bushy place. Bh is pronounced as w.

WALLTOWER. Town on a steep abrupt hill. *Bhaile, baile* aspirated, town; *torr*, steep hill. *Bhaile* is pronounced wall-e or, with e dropped, wall

WALLYFORD. Ford at a town. *Bhaile, baile* aspirated, town. Bh is equal to w.

WALSTONE. Town at a stone. *Bhaile, baile* aspirated, town *Bhaile* is pronounced wall-e, and final e in names is usually lost. Stone might represent ton, town, with s prefixed to obtain a possessive.

WANTON WA'S, WANTON WELLS. Town at a fold. *Bhaile, baile* aspirated, town; *chuitail, cuitail* aspirated, fold. *Bhaile* became waile, afterwards made wall, to which s was added for euphony, and walls became wa's and wells. *Chuitail* was corrupted into whitehill, which was made in Gaelic *bhandun*, white hill (*bhan, ban* aspirated, white; *dun*, hill), now become wanton. Wanton Wa's and Wanton Wells are not uncommon names.

WARDIE. Little meadow. *Bhardan, bardan* aspirated, little meadow. Bh is equivalent to w, and an normally became i

WARKLAW Hill with a conspicuous summit. *Torr*, hill, *bharrach, barrach* aspirated, over-topping. Bh is equal to v.

WARRISTON, for *Baile Bharra*. Town on a point *Baile*, town ; *bharra*, *barra* aspirated, *point*. Bh is equal to w

WATHERSTON, for *Baile Bheath Airidh* Town at a birch-wood on a shieling. *Baile*, town , *bheath*, *beath* aspirated, birch-wood ; *airidh*, shieling Bh is equal to w, and idh is silent.

WAULKMILL. Mill where cloth is felted by beating. Originally cloth was felted by people walking on it while wet.

WEATHER LAW Hill of the shieling where birches grow. *Lamh*, hill , *airidh* (idh silent), shieling ; *bheath*, *beath* aspirated, birch-wood. Bh is equal to w

WEDALE, for *Chuidail*. Fold. *Chuidail*, *cuidail* aspirated, fold. Ch had become silent and had been lost, leaving uidail, which became wedale. Wedale is an old name for the parish now called Stow.

WELL OF SPA Well whose water is impregnated with carbonate of iron. The name had been imported from Spa in Belgium, where there are chalybeate springs.

WELLHEADS, for *Bhaile Chuidan*. Town at a small fold *Bhaile*, *baile* aspirated, town ; *chuidan*, *cuidan* aspirated, little fold. Bh is equal to w and *bhaile* became waile, and by loss of final e it became well. C in ch is silent and had been lost. An became s instead of ie, which produced huids, now heads

WELLINGTON INN. If this name is Gaelic it means inn at a corner *Uileann*, nook, angle

WETHOLM, for *Tolm Chuit*. Hill of the fold. *Tolm*, round hillock , *chuit*, *cuit* aspirated, fold. Ch became silent and was lost, and uit became wet. The parts of the name had been transposed, and *tolm* became *tholm*.

WHAUPHILL, for *Chop* Hill. Hill *Chop*, *cop* aspirated, hill. The name looks as if it meant hill of the curlew, but curlews frequent many hills in the county of Edinburgh.

WHEATFIELD, for White field The original form had been *Achadh Chuit*. Field of the fold. *Achadh*, field ; *chuit*, *cuit* aspirated, fold *Chuit* had been corrupted into white when Gaelic was passing into Scotch

WHELPSIDE, for *Suidhe Coillean*. Place on a little hill. *Suidhe*, place ; *coillean*, little hill. *Coillean* had been supposed to be *cuilean*, little dog, and had been made whelp in English

WHINNYHAUGH. Haugh where assemblies were held. *Choinne*, coinne aspirated, meeting

WHIPPIE LAW, for *Choipean Lamh* Little hill *Choipean*, *coipean* aspirated, little hill , *lamh*, hill. *Coipean* is a diminutive from *coip*, genitive of *cop*, hill Ch had become wh, and an had become ie.

WHISTLEGATE, for *Tulach Gaothach Chois* Hill of the windy gap. *Tulach*, hill, round knoll , *gaothach*, windy . *chois*, genitive aspirated of *cos*, hollow

WHITE. Fold. *Chuit*, *cuit* aspirated, fold, corrupted into white.

The following names were also originally *Chuit*, etc. :—

WHITE CLEUGH. Fold in a ravine with steep sides. Cleugh, steep bank, ravine.

WHITE HOUSE. Fold. *Chuith, cuith* aspirated, fold. C had been lost, and th had become sh, which lost h. Huis was left and it became house.

WHITE MOSS. Moss of the fold.

WHITE SYKES. Small streams draining a wet place at a fold.

WHITEFAUGH. Field of the fold. Faugh, cultivated land.

WHITELEA Grass-land at a fold.

WHITESIDE LAW. Hill of the site of a fold. *Lamh*, hill ; *suidhe*, site

WHITE HILL, WHITEHILL. Fold. *Chuitail, cuitail* aspirated, fold, corrupted into white hill and whitehill.

The following names also began originally with *Chuitail*, which became whitehill, but hill was subsequently turned into Gaelic in various ways. .—

WHITE CRAIG HEADS. Hill became *creag*, hill, now made craig. Heads is for *chuidan, cuidan* aspirated, little fold. C was lost and an was made s instead of ie. Huids has now become heads.

WHITE LUMS, WHITELUMS. Hill became *lamhan*, diminutive of *lamh*, hill. An became s, improperly, producing lamhs, now lums.

WHITE RIG. Hill became *ruigh*, slope, hill, now rig.

WHITEBURGH. Hill became *bruch*, hill, now burgh.

WHITEHOPE. Hill became *chop, cop* aspirated, hill. C was lost, and e was added.

WHITELAW. Hill became *lamh*, hill, in which mh is equal to w.

WHOLE STOCK. Hill sustaining cattle. *Coille*, hill ; *stoc*, cattle, wealth.

WILKIES WOOD, WILKIESTON. Wood in a corner, and Town in a corner *Uileann*, nook, angle. Eann had become ie, and k had been inserted in the belief that uilie was the diminutive of William.

WILLIAMSTON. Town at a crook in a burn. *Uileann*, nook, crook, corner.

WINCHEL HILL. The three parts of the name mean the same thing. The first had been *bheinn, beinn*, aspirated, hill, pronounced wane. The second had been *choill, coill* aspirated, hill, now made chel. Winchel in English names probably means hill.

WINDY MAINS, for *Gaothach Man*. Windy Hill. *Gaothach*, windy ; *man*, hill. S represents an of *man*, supposed to be a plural termination.

WINDY DOOR NICK, for *Gaothach Dorus na Eag*. Windy door in the gap. *Gaothach*, windy ; *dorus*, door, gap ; *na*, of the ; *eag*, notch, gap.

WINDYDOORS HAWSE. Windy gap. Doors is for *dorus*, door, gap; hawse is an English word meaning throat or neck.

WISP. Bush of trees.

WITCHES SYKE. Drain from a small fold. *Chuithan, cuithan* aspirated, small fold. Ch was lost, an became es instead of ie, and th was strengthened by the insertion of c, producing uitches, now witches. Syke (Scotch) means a very small stream.

WOLF CLEUGH. Cliff haunted by a wolf. But wolf might be a corruption of *uamh*, pronounced uav, cave.

WOODCOT, for *Coill Cuit.* Hill of the fold. *Coill*, hill, translated into wood by mistake, *cuit*, fold. See Woodhall.

WOODHALL. Hill. Wood had originally been *coill*, hill, which had been translated into wood, the modern meaning of *coill*; the second part, hall, had been *choill, coill* aspirated, hill, added to the first to explain it after being translated. *Choill* lost c, and oi became a.

WOODHOUSELEE. Grass-land on the hill of the fold. Wood, translation of *coill*, hill, *chuith, cuith* aspirated, fold; ley (Scotch), grass-land. See Woodhall and Turnhouse.

WOOLMET, for *Uileann Meud* Big corner, wide nook. *Uileann*, corner, *meud*, greatness.

WOOLY LAW, for *Lamh Uileann* Hill in an angle between two burns. *Lamh*, hill; *uileann*, angle, corner.

WRIGHTS HOUSES, for *Sealan Airidh.* Shiels on summer pasture *Sealan*, shiels, huts; *airidh*, hill pasture. Before cultivated fields were fenced cattle had to be sent to hill pastures in summer, and houses built of sods were provided for mistresses of families and their children, for women to milk cows, and for men to herd the cattle.

WULL MUIR. Moor in a corner, where there is a turn in a road *Uileann*, nook, corner. Eann became ie, which was lost.

YANCRUM. The fold *An*, the, *crom*, circle, fold.

YELLOWSTRUTHER, for *Sruth Chuit Airidh.* Burn of the fold on a shieling. *Sruth*, burn, *chuit, cuit* aspirated, fold; *airidh*, shieling. *Chuit* was corrupted into white, which was turned into Gaelic again by *gealach*, white. *Gealach* was corrupted into yellow, gh being equal to y. Yellow was put first because it was supposed to be an English adjective.

YORKSTON. Quiet town. *Iorrach*, quiet.

PLACE NAMES

OF

EAST LOTHIAN

GAELIC
PLACE NAMES
OF
EAST LOTHIAN

BY

JOHN MILNE, LL.D.

PUBLISHED FOR THE AUTHOR BY

M^cDOUGALL'S EDUCATIONAL COMPANY, LIMITED.

LONDON : 8 FARRINGDON AVENUE, E.C.

EDINBURGH : 1 AND 2 ST. JAMES SQUARE.

PLACE NAMES OF
EAST LOTHIAN.

———◉———

ABERLADY. Mouth of the broad estuary of the Peffer Burn *Aber*, infall; *leathan*, broad. Th became dh, and h was afterwards lost. An became y though not a diminutive termination

ADNISTON. Town on a hill. *Aodann*, brae, hill. Ann is a diminutive termination and had been changed to ie, now i. Some had regarded it as a plural termination and had made it s, and thus it represents ann in two ways.

AFRICA, for *Ruigh Abh.* Slope going down to a burn. *Ruigh*, slope; *abh*, burn, water

AIKENGALL. Stone at a fold   *Gall*, rock, stone pillar; *aigheann*, fold.

AIKIESIDE   Site of a fold. *Aigheann*, fold; *suidhe*, place

ALDERSTON. Alder is for *Aill Der*, little hill. *Aill*, hill, *der* (Irish), small.   Ton represents *dun*, an addition made to explain *aill*

ALLER BOG.   Alder bog.

AMISFIELD.   Field of shooting at a mark.   *Amusadh*, aiming.

ANNFIELD.   Enclosed field   *Innis*, enclosure.

ARCHERFIELD. High land field.   *Ard*, hill, *thir*, *tir* aspirated, land.   *Tir* was aspirated because it follows its adjective.

ASCENSION. Little burn of the hill. *Easan*, little burn, *sithean* (th silent), hill.

ASHYHAUGH.   Haugh of the little burn.   *Easan*, small burn; *Eas* became ash, and an normally became y.

ATHELSTANEFORD, for *Ath Clach Aoil.* Limestone kiln.   *Ath*, kiln; *clach*, stone; *aoil*, lime   There is in Gaelic a word *ath*, kiln; and there is also another *ath*, ford   By a mistake the translation of the second *ath* had been added to the name to explain the first *ath* at the beginning   There is no limestone at Athelstaneford but there is to the west.   It had been conveyed to Athelstaneford and had been burned in a kiln there.

BACK O' LINGHOPE.   Round backed ridge near Linghope. On the Ordnance Survey map this name is placed on the top of the ridge between two burn ravines called Ling Hope and Wide Hope   By hope is apparently meant a ravine or sheltered place, whereas hope in Gaelic names means hill.

BACK RIG.   Round backed ridge between two ravines. *Ruigh* (erroneously supposed to mean ridge), slope of a hill.

B

BAILIE'S HAG WOOD. Jackdaw's wood at a farm town. *Baile*, town; *chathag, cathag* aspirated, jackdaw. *Chathag* lost c and tha. *Cathag* (th silent) is an imitation of the cry of the bird.

BALGONE Town of the fold. *Baile*, town; *gabhann* (bh equal ou), fold.

BANGLY HILL. Hill of the fold. *Chuitail, cuitail* aspirated, fold. *Chuitail* became whitehill, which was turned into Gaelic by *banlamh*, white hill (*ban*, white; *lamh*, hill). Euphonic g had been added to an, and mh had been lost.

BANK. Fold. *Chuit, cuit* aspirated, fold. *Chuit* became white, which was made in Gaelic *ban*, white, with euphonic k added.

BANK BURN. Burn of the fold. *Chuit, cuit* aspirated, fold, corrupted into white, which was turned into Gaelic by *ban*, white, with the addition of euphonic k.

BANKHEAD. Fold. The first part of the name had originally been *chuit, cuit* aspirated, fold, which had been corrupted into white. White had again been turned into Gaelic by *ban*, white, to which k had been added for euphony. The second part had been added to explain the first after it had been corrupted. Head is *chuid, cuid* aspirated, fold, in which c being silent, had been lost. Huid had been pronounced heed, which has now become head.

BANKHEAD (Prestonpans). Head of level terrace.

BANKRUGG. Fold. *Chuitail, cuitail* aspirated, fold, corrupted into whitehill, which was made *banruigh*, white hill (*ban*, white; *ruigh*, hill). K is a euphonic addition to n.

BARA. Point. *Barra*, point, court, place where barony courts were held.

BARBERFIELD. Field at the point of a spit of land. *Barr*, point; *bear*, spit.

BARD. Meadow.

BAREBANES, for *Bear Beannan* Point of the little hill. *Bear*, point; *beannan*, little hill. An improperly became es instead of ie.

BARNESS. Gap. *Bearnas* (Irish), gap.

BARNEY HILL, BARNY HILL. Hill showing a gap in the sky line. *Bearna* (Irish), gap.

BARNS. Place in a hollow. *Bearnas*, gap, hollow.

BARRACKS. A place at a higher elevation than others near it. *Barrachas*, superiority.

BASS. Death. The Bass rock had formerly been a place of execution.

BATHAN'S STRAND. Little hollow filled with a small arm of the sea *Bathan*, diminutive of *bath*, sea; *srathan*, small valley, low place. Final s in Bathan's is a mistake for ie D is a euphonic addition to an.

BATHE. Cow-byre. *Bathaich*, cow-byre. Ch had been lost.

BAXTER SYKE. Drain from a big cliff. *Bagach*, big; *stor*,

cliff. *Bagach* by losing ach became bag in bag-rope, the term for a thick rope round the eave of a rick. X in Baxster should be g.

BEANSTON. Hill town. *Beinn*, hill, S represents einn.

BEARFORD. Burn ford. *Bior*, water, burn

BEATTIE'S ROW. Row of houses where birches grow *Beathach*, abounding in birch-trees. Beattie's might be a personal name.

BEESKNOWE, for *Beith* Knowe. Knoll growing birches. *Beith*, birch.

BEGBIE Small birch wood *Beag*, small; *beith*, birch, birch-wood.

BEIL. Mouth of a stream. *Beil*, second form of *beul*, mouth.

BELHAVEN. Mouth of the burn *Beil*, mouth; *abhainn*, stream *Beil* is a second form of *beul*, mouth. Euphonic h had been prefixed to *abhainn*.

BELL, BELL CRAIG, BELL'S CRAIG, BELL'S WOOD, BELLYFORD, BELTON, BELTON DOD. The first part of the names is *buaile*, fold. S is the English possessive sign Craig is *creag*, hill; ton is town, and dod is a corruption of *cnoc*, hill.

BENNET'S BURN. Burn of the hill. *Beinn*, hill; *netan*, small burn. An ought to have become ie, not s.

BENT WOOD. Wood on a hill. *Beinn*, hill, with euphonic t added.

BERRY HILL. Watery Hill. *Biorach*, watery. Several streams flow from this hill

BERWICK. Sharp point at a nook. *Bear*, spit, *uig*, nook, cove

BETONY HILL. Hill abounding in birches. *Beuthanach*, producing birches

BEUGH BURN. Roaring burn. *Beuchach*, noisy, roaring.

BILSDEAN Den of the fold. *Buaile*, fold, *dein*, den.

BINNING. Little hill. *Beinnan*, diminutive of *beinn*, hill

BIRLIE KNOWE. Knoll on the projecting point of a hill. *Cnocan*, diminutive of *cnoc*, hill, *beur*, point; *lamh*, hill. *Cnocan* has assumed various forms in Scotch—knockie, knox, knoll, knowe, knollys, knowles. In knockie an normally became ie; in knox it abnormally became s, which combining with c made x; in knoll and knowe an was lost, in knollys it became both y, normally, and ies, abnormally. In knoll and knollys c disappeared and ll took its place, and when ll was lost o became ow. In knowles oll has become owl.

BIRNIEKNOWES, BIRNY KNOWE Knoll of the gap. *Cnocan*, knoll; *bearna* (Irish), gap. An had by a mistake been regarded as plural and made s

BIRNS WATER Burn flowing in a gap. *Bearnas* (Irish), gap.

BIRSET HILL. Hill abounding in bushes. *Preasach*, bushy place.

BIRSLIE BRAE. Brae of the bushy hill. *Preas*, bush ; *lamh*, hill.

BLACK CASTLE, BLACK KNOWE, BLACK LAW, BLAKELAW, BLACKMAINS. Black and Blake represent *Bleoghann*, milking, with gh hardened into ch. Blake is nearer the original, k only being inserted. Ann though not a diminutive termination here had been made ie, which had afterwards being lost, being final. The fold at Black Castle had been mistaken for a fort. Law is *lamh*, hill. Mains is *man*, hill, with a added because it ended in an, but it is not here a plural termination. It became mains because it was a farm name.

BLACK GRAIN. Black burn which joins another burn.

BLACK MURPHIES, for *Mor Chuith Bleoghann*. Big fold for milking cows　*Mor*, big ; *chuith, cuith* aspirated, fold ; *bleoghann*, milking. Ch had become ph, and th had become sh and afterwards s. Ann is not a diminutive termination here but it had been made ie, which being final had been lost. Black in names often refers to milk and milking.

BLADDERING CLEUGH. Ravine of the milking-fold, on a small shieling. *Bleodhann*, milking-place ; *airidhean*, small shieling. Ann improperly became ie, which was lost. G had been added to final n of *airidhean*.

BLAIKIE HEUGH. Milking fold at a steep bank. *Bleoghann*, milking.

BLANCE. Small warm place. *Blathan* (th silent), diminutive of *blath*, warm. An abnormally became s, now ce.

BLAWEARIE, for *Blath Chuith Airidh*. Pleasant fold on the shieling. *Blath*, warm, pleasant ; *chuith, cuith* aspirated, fold ; *airidh*, shieling　All the aspirated letters were lost. Ui is pronounced we.

BLEAK LAW　Hill of the milking fold　*Bleoghann*, milking ; *lamh*, hill.

BLINDWALLS, for *Bailean Caoch*. Little town on a burn. *Bailean*, diminutive of *baile*, town ; *caoch*, burn. *Caoch* had been supposed to be the adjective *caoch*, blind. *Bailean* had been made *bhailean*, and put last. Bh is equal to w, and ean had by mistake been made s. Bhails became first wails and then walls.

BLINDWELL BRAE, for Brae of the well of the little burn. *Caoch*, blind, and *caoch*, burn, had been confounded together in the name. Two mistakes had been made, one in making *caoch*, blind, instead of burn, and the other in making the well blind. In the Hebrew language a well is regarded as an eye, and a dry well might be called blind in Hebrew, but not in English.

BLINKBONNY. Milking fold in a howe. *Bleoghann*, milking-place ; *bonnan*, little bottom, howe.

BLINKIE BURN, for *Cuith Bleoghann*. Fold where cows were milked. *Cuith* (th silent), fold ; *bleoghann* (gh silent), milking.

BLOODY SIDE. Milking place. *Bleodhann*, milking ; *suidhe*, place. Ann become y, abnormally.

BLUEHOLES. Hillock where cows were milked. *Choillean, coillean* aspirated, little hill; *bleoghann,* milking. C of *choillean* was lost, and ean was made es instead of ie. Ann of *bleoghann* had become ie and had been lost.

BLUEHOUSES. Little milking fold. *Bleoghann,* milking; *chuithan, cuithan* aspirated, little fold. Gh is equal to y, and ann had become ie, which had been lost. C in ch had been lost, th had become sh and afterwards s, and an abnormally became es.

BOAR STONE. Big stone   *Borr,* great

BOAR'S CLEUGH   Big cleugh   *Borr,* big

BOGGS, for *Bogan.* Soft moist place   *Bogan,* diminutive of *bog,* wet, marshy place. An was improperly made s.

BOGLEHILL   Cow-stall hill. *Buaigheal,* cow-stall.

BOHOMY, for *Both Thoman*   House on the little hill   *Both* (th silent), house, *thoman, toman* aspirated, hill. T in *thoman* is silent, and an had become y, normally.

BOLTON. Town at a fold. *Buaile,* fold.

BONETTY KNOWE   Bottom of the knoll near a litttle burn. *Bonn,* bottom; *netan,* little burn; *cnocan,* diminutive of *cnoc,* hill. An normally became y.

BONNINGTON. Town in a little hollow (at the foot of North Berwick Law)   *Bonnan,* diminutive of *bonn,* bottom, hollow.

BONNY WOOD. Wood in the bottom of a valley. *Bonnan,* little hollow. An normally became y

BOONSLY SHANK. Hill of the quarry. *Buidhinn,* quarry; *lamh,* hill   Shank is *sithean,* hill, with euphonic k added, an explanation of ly the corruption of *lamh.* All the aspirated letters had been lost, being silent. S in Boonsly represents inn, improperly regarded as a plural termination.

BOTHER CLEUGH, BOTHER STONE   *Bother* represents *Both Airidh*   House on a shieling. *Both,* hut, shiel, *airidh,* shieling.

BOTHWELL. House at a farm town. *Both,* house, *bhaile, baile* aspirated, farm town. Bh is equal to w, and waile became well.

BOWERHOUSE   Cattlefold. *Buar,* cattle; *chuith, cuith* aspirated, fold. C in ch is silent. Th became sh, which became s by loss of h, and then huis became house

BOY'S BUSS   Yellow snout. *Buidhe,* yellow; *bus,* snout, rock like a snout. S represents the sound of dhe.

BRAID LAW. Both parts mean hill. *Braid* (Irish), hill; *lamh,* hill.

BRAIDBUS HILL   Hill of the snout   *Braid,* hill; *bus,* snout.

BRAND'S MILL. Mill on a burn. *Braon,* hill burn   S represents aon.

BRANSLYSHIEL. House on the hill of the burn. *Seal,* shiel, residence on summer pasture, *lamh,* hill; *braon,* hill burn   S represents aon

BRANXTON. Town on a little burn. *Braonan*, diminutive of *braon*, burn. Euphonic c had been added to *braon*, and final an had abnormally been made s. C and s combined made x.

BROAD LECKS. Broad flat rocks. *Leacan*, plural of *leac*, flat slab.

BROOK BURN. Hill burn. *Bruch*, hill.

BRODIE'S FOLD. Fold at a sharp corner. *Brodan*, point. S represents an, erroneously regarded as a plural termination.

BROOKSIDE. Place on a hill. *Bruch*, hill; *suidhe*, place.

BROOMHOUSE. Fold at a place growing broom. House represents *chuith*, *cuith* aspirated, fold. C of ch became silent and was lost; th became sh and h was lost, leaving huis, now house.

BROWN DOD. Hill of the burn. *Cnoc*, hill; *braon*, mountain burn.

BROWNRIGG, BROWNRIG. Place sloping to a burn. *Braon*, burn; *ruigh*, slope.

BROWN'S PLACE. Place at a burn. *Braon*, burn. S represents aon.

BROWNSHILL. Hill of the mountain burn. *Braon*, burn. S had been put in because *braon* ended in aon.

BRUCE'S CIRCLE. Circle on a small hill. *Bruchan*, small hill. An abnormally became s instead of ie.

BRUNT HILL. Hill of the burn. *Braon*, burn.

BUBBLY BUSS. Rock of lamentation *Bubail*, lamentation; *bus*, snout. The rock had caused loss of life in storms.

BUGHT KNOWE. Knoll where there was a house for sheep. *Buth*, hut for sheep. Th had become gh, and t had been added for euphony

BUGHTS. Houses for sheep. *Buth*, hut. Th became gh, to which t was added for euphony.

BUIST'S EMBANKMENT. Dyke made to retain mud and exclude the sea. *Buiste*, pocket, pouch.

BULLHOPE LAW. Hill of the fold. *Chop*, *cop* aspirated, hill; *buaile*, fold; *lamh*, hill. The last part is a recent addition.

BURLAGE QUARRY. Quarry on an open moor on a hill. *Blair*, open place, *aod*, hill, brae. *Blair* by transposition of letters became baril, which was made burl. D is sometimes pronounced as dg, and *aod* became age.

BURN HOPE. Burn of the hill. *Chop*, *cop* aspirated, hill. C silent had been dropped.

BURNFOOT. Fold at a burn. *Chuit*, *cuit* aspirated, fold; *braon*, hill burn. Ch became ph, which is f.

BURNING MOUNT, for *Braonan Monadh*. Little burn from a hill. *Braonan*, diminutive of *braon*, burn; *monadh*, hill, moor.

BUSHELHILL. Hill of the shepherd. *Buachaille*, shepherd.

BUTTERDEAN, for *Dein Buth Airidh*. Den of the hut on the shieling. *Dein*, den; *buth*, hut, shiel; *airidh*, summer pasture, shieling.

BUXLEY. Big grassy place. *Buchd*, bulk, big , *ley* (Scotch), grass-land. X is not a Gaelic letter, and in Buxley it must represent some combination of other letters. The name might mean a farm all in pasture. In Scotch bulk, pronounced book, means the whole of a thing.

BYRIE HILL. Pointed hill. *Biorach*, pointed.

CAERLAVEROCK. Slope of the shieling hill. *Ruigh*, slope ; *cathair* (th silent), hill , *lamh*, hill ; *airidh*, shieling *Cathair* had been prefixed to *lamh* as an explanation after its meaning had been lost. Though *lamh*, hill, is in many names no Irish or Gaelic dictionary gives it.

CAIRN HILL. Hill. *Carn*, hill. The second part is a translation of the first.

CAIRNDINNIS. Hill of the little hill. *Carn*, hill; *dunan*, little hill An had become both ie and s.

CALDER CLEUGH. Ravine of the rapid river. *Cleugh*, ravine ; *callaidh*, active , *dobhar* (bh silent), water.

CAMPTON Town at a camp The supposed camp was the pumphal or cattlefold called The Chesters.

CAMY CLEUGH. Ravine with curves. *Camach*, crooked.

CANTY BAY. Bay of the little head *Ceanntan*, diminutive of *ceann*, head. An normally became y.

CANTYHALL. Little hill. *Ceanntan*, little hill; *choill*, *coill* aspirated, hill. *Ceanntan* is *ceannan*, diminutive of *ceann*, head, with euphonic t inserted. Final an normally became y.

CAR. Turn in the line of the coast. *Car*, turn, bend. Or, Projecting shelf of rock. *Carr*, projecting point. Both meanings are appropriate.

CARFRAE Hill of heather. *Cathair* (th silent), hill ; *fraoch* (och silent), heather

CARLEKEMP. Hill with a crooked side. *Cathair* (th silent), hill ; *leth* (th silent), side , *cam*, crooked, with euphonic p added to m.

CARPERSTANE, perhaps for *Carr Chnap Airidh*. Monumental pillar on the highest point of a shieling. *Carr*, monumental stone ; *chnap*, *cnap* aspirated, knoll, knap , *airidh* shieling. Ch is often silent and liable to be lost, and n after c is often lost, as in cock for *cnoc*. Stane is a translation of *carr*.

CASTLE MOFFAT. Big fold, erroneously supposed to have been a castle. *Mo*, great , *chuit*, *cuit* aspirated, fold. Ch became ph, equal to f.

CASTLE SHOT Field at Norham Castle *Sgot*, spot, small field.

CASTLE TARBET Place like a castle on a rock separated from Fidra Island. *Tearbta*, separated.

CAT CRAIG. Hill at a road *Creag*, hill , *cat*, road

CATIE CLEUGH. Steep bank where there is a path *Catha*, drove road, path.

CAUL. Place where a river is narrowed by a wall projecting into it. *Caol*, narrow Here the wall had been carried across the river and had been made a weir.

CAULD BURN. Slender Burn. *Caol*, narrow, with euphonic d added to l. Silent d is often found after l.

CAULDRAW, for *Rath Cuil*. Fold in a nook. *Rath*, circle, fold , *cuil*, nook.

CAULDSHIEL. Shiel in a corner. *Cuil*, nook ; *seal*, temporary summer residence.

CAULDSIDE. North-lying place, *Cul*, back, north ; *suidhe*, place.

CHALMERS'S BUSSHEAD, for *Bus Chuid Sealbhar*. Rock which had served as a fold for cattle. *Bus*, rock like a snout , *chuid*, *cuid* aspirated, fold ; *sealbhar*, cattle. Since bh and mh are both sounded v they are often confounded, and so also are b and m. Se is equal to she in Gaelic, and *sealbhar* had become chalmer.

CHARLIE'S PLANTATION. Plantation at a dark fold. *Sear*, (pronounced shear), black, dark ; *lios*, fold.

CHARTERIS'S WELL. Well on a black shieling. *Sear*, dark ; *airidh*, shieling.

CHESTER HILL, CHESTERHALL, CHESTERHILL. Hill of the sunny land. *Deas*, south, sunny, sometimes east; *choill*, *coill* aspirated, hill

CHESTERS, an ancient cattlefold surrounded by concentric dykes and ditches for defence against cattle thieves (See "Douglas, a Tragedy "). There are within the enclosure traces of byres for cows which were milked night and morning. Chesters is a recent name derived from the Latin word *castra*, camp. *Castra* is plural, therefore s had been added to chester.

CINDERHALL, for *Choill Sithean Airidh*. Hill of the shieling. *Choill*, *coill* aspirated, hill ; *sithean* (thea silent), hill ; *airidh*, shieling. Euphonic d had been added to cin for sin.

CLACHERDEAN. Den of the stepping stones. *Dein*, den ; *clacharan*, stepping stones. An had been lost by becoming ie.

CLARTYSIDE. Beautiful place. *Clardha*, beautiful ; *suidhe*, place.

CLAY KNOWE. Knoll composed.of clay ; but clay may be a corruption of *clachach*, stony.

CLECKMAY. Fold of wattled work in a plain. *Cleath*, wattled fold ; *magh*, plain. Th had become ch, afterwards made ck. Gh is equal to y.

CLERKINGTON, for *Baile Claran*. Town at a small open clear place. *Baile*, town ; *claran*, diminutive of *clar*, open smooth place. Euphonic k had been added to r.

CLINTS DOD. See Clints Law, and Dod.

CLINTS LAW, for *Cleathan Lamh*. Hill of the little fold. *Lamh*, hill ; *cleathan* (th silent), little fold. T is a euphonic addition to n, and s had been added in the mistaken belief that *cleathan* was plural.

CLOVERY ROAD. Stony road. *Clocharra*, stoney. Ch became bh, equal to v.

COALSTON. Hill town. *Coill*, hill.

COATIEBURN. Burn at the litttle fold *Cuitan*, small fold. An normally became ie.

COCKBURN. Hill burn. *Cnoc*, hill.

COCKENZIE, for *Cnoc Fhaingan* Hill of the small fank. *Cnoc*, hill, *fhaingan*, *faingan* aspirated, small fank *Faingan* is a second form of *fangan*, small fold. Fh is silent and had been lost.

COCKIELAW. Small hill. *Cnocan*, small hill, with an normally changed to ie; *lamh*, hill.

COCKLAW HILL. Hill. *Cnoc*, hill, *lamh*, hill.

COCKLES BRAE, for *Cnoc Aillean*. Little hill. *Cnoc*, hill, *aillean*, diminutive of *aill*, hill. *Cnoc* had lost n, and ean of *aillean* had become s instead of ie.

COCKSTON STEEL. Burn of the little hill. *Steall*, spring gushing out; *cnocan*, diminutive of *cnoc*, hill; *dun*, hill. An had become s instead of ie.

COCMILANE, for *Cnoc Millan* Little hill *Cnoc*, hill; *millan*, diminutive of *mill*, second form of *meall*, hill. *Cnoc* is a late addition to explain *millan*, but it too had been corrupted and had lost n

COGTAIL. This name had originallly been *Cuitail*, fold, in which *cuit* means fold. *Cog*, which also means fold, had been substituted for *cuit*.

COLDALE. Hill field *Choill*, *coill* aspirated, hill, *dail*, riverside field.

COLDHAME. Back of the hill *Cul*, back; *thom*, *tom* aspirated, hill. T in *thom* is silent and had been lost.

COLLAR LAW. Hill of the shieling. *Coill*, hill; *airidh*, shieling; *lamh*, hill. *Lamh* is a late addition explaining the corrupted name.

COLLEGEHEAD, for *Chuid Aod Coill* Fold on the brae of a hill. *Chuid*, *cuid* aspirated, fold, *aod*, brae; *coill*, hill. When *cuid* became *chuid* and then head it had been put last. D is often sounded as dg in Gaelic.

COLLISON'S BENCH Shelf on a hill *Coille*, hill; *sithean*, hill. Th with the adjacent vowels had been lost, and san became son.

COMMON HOUSE. Common fold. *Chuith*, *cuith* aspirated, fold. C in ch is silent, th became first sh and then s by loss of the aspirate. Huis became house.

CONGALTON. Town. *Congbhail*, town, habitation

COOPER'S CLOSE Enclosure on a shieling hill. *Cop*, hill; *airidh*, shieling.

CORBY WELL, CORBY CRAIGS. Well at a fold, and Rocks at a fold. Corby was originally *Chuitail*, *cuitail* aspirated, fold, which was corrupted into whitehill. This was turned into Gaelic by *corban*, white hill (*cor*, hill; *ban*, white) An had been mistaken for a diminutive termination and had been changed to y, producing corby Folds were usually near wells or burns. Craigs is for *creagan*, plural of *creag*, rock, hill.

CORSEHOUSE. Fold at a crossing of roads *Crois*, cross;

chuith, cuith aspirated, fold. Ch lost c, and th became sh, and by loss of the aspirate it was made s. Huis lapsed into house.

CORSICK HILL. Hill of the crossing. *Creag*, crossing.

COSTERTON   Town on land in a howe. *Cos*, hollow; *tir*, land.

COT CLEUGH, COW CLEUGH. Ravine of the fold. *Cuit*, fold, *cuith* (th silent), fold.

COW STRAND. Glen of the fold *Srathan*, diminutive of *srath*, flat-bottomed alluvial river valley; *cuith*, fold   Th is silent and had been lost. Euphonic d had been added to an.

COWIE LAW. Little hill. *Coillean*, little hill. When ll is lost a preceding o or oi becomes ow.

COWTHROPLE   Goodlooking fold   *Cuith* (th silent), fold; *triopollach*, (Irish), trim, proper.

COWTON RIDGE, COWTON ROCKS. Cowton is *cuidan*, small fold. The names indicate that the sea has encroached upon the land.

CRACKING SHAW. Bushy place on a hill. *Creachan*, small hill.

CRAIG, CRAIG BURN, CRAIG KNOWE, CRAIGLEITH, CRAIGMOOR. Craig is *creag*, hill. Knowe is *cnocan*, diminutive of *cnoc*, hill, with final c silent and an changed to e. Leith is *liath*, grey.

CRAIGANTEUCH. Smooth little rock. *Creagan*, little rock; *teith* (Irish), smooth. Th had become ch.

CRAGIELAW. Both parts mean hill, law having been added to explain Craigie after it had been corrupted. *Creagan*, small hill; *lamh*, hill.

CRAIG'S QUARRY. Quarry in a little hill. *Creagan*, small hill.

CRAIGY HILL. Little hill. *Creagan*, little hill.

CRANCHIE. Full of trees. *Craobhach* (bh equal u), woody.

CRIB BURN. Burn at a fold. *Crubh*, fold.

CRICHNESS. Point of the hill. *Ness*, nose, point; *creach*, hill In Gaelic *ness* is pronounced nish.

CROCKERS HEDGES, for *Aodann Cnoc Airidh*   Brae of the hill of the shieling. *Aodann*, brae; *cnoc*, hill; *airidh*. H was prefixed to *aodann*, and ann was by mistake made es. *Aod* sounds edg.

CROMWELLHALL   Hill of the town at a fold. *Choill, coill* aspirated, hill; *bhaile, baile* aspirated, town; *crom*, fold. C being lost, hoill became hall. Bh is equal to w and *bhaile* became well.

CROOK. Hill. *Cnoc*, hill. N preceded by c often became r.

CROSS HILL. Place of crossing a hill. *Crasg*, crossing.

CROSS KEYS. Small fold where a road crossed a boundary *Cuithan*, small fold. Th, being silent, was lost, and an was improperly changed to s instead of ie.

CROSSGATEHALL. Hill of the windy crossing. *Choill, coill* aspirated, hill; *crois*, cross-roads; *gaothach*, wind. C of *choill* was lost, and oi became a

CROW CLEUGH, CROW HILL, CROWHILL, CROW ISLAND, CROW MOSS, CROW STONES. Crow is *cro*, wattled fold.

CROWN WOOD. Round wood. *Cruinn*, round.

CRYSTAL RIG. Slope of the little fold on the hill *Ruigh*, slope, shieling; *crudhan*, small fold; *aill*, hill. Db is equal to y, and an had improperly been made s

CUDDIE WOOD, CUDDY NEUK Small fold. *Cuidan*, small fold. An normally became ie and y.

CUTHILL. Fold. *Cuithail*, fold.

DALGOWRIE Field of the goats. *Dail*, field near a stream; *gabharach*, used for goats.

DALSKELLY CRAIGS. Field near rocks. *Dail*, field; *sgeilgean*, plural of *sgeilg*, rock; *creagan*, plural of *creag*, rock.

DANSKINE LOCH. Loch at the head of two burns. *Cinn*, second form of *ceann*, head; *da*, two; *abhainn*, burn. *Da* and *abhainn* contracted became dan, and an of dan was made s.

DARNED HOUSE. Fold at a ford over a burn. *Chuith, cuith* aspirated, fold; *darn*, ford; *ned*, burn C silent was lost, th became sh, and h was lost. Huis became house.

DAW'S WELL. Well of the jackdaw Daw, name imitating the cry of the bird Or, Well of the deer. *Damh*, stag, red deer. Mh is sounded u, v, or w.

DEAD GRAIN. Black branch of a burn. *Dubh*, black. Bh and dh are both equal to y, hence b and d had been confused

DELVES. Small statue of a man. *Dealbhan*, diminutive of *dealbh*, figure, statue. An had improperly become es

DEUCHRIE DOD, DEUCHRIE EDGE. Hill of the black slope. *Dubh*, black; *ruigh*, slope; Dod and Edge both mean hill. Dod is a corruption of *cnoc*, hill, and Edge is a corruption of *aod*, brae, hill Dh of *dubh* became ch.

DINGLETON. Town on a hill where there is a monumental stone pillar. *Dun*, hill; *gall*, monumental pillar.

DIRLETON. Small town. *Direoil*, small.

DIRTSIDE Place on a brae. *Suidhe*, place; *direadh*, ascent

DISHUP HA', for *Deas Chop Choill*. Sunny side of the hill. *Deas* (pronounced dash), south, sunny, *chop*, *cop* aspirated, hill; *choill, coill* aspirated, hill Ch in *chop* had become silent and had been lost. C in *choill* had been lost, hoill had become hall, and subsequently ll had been lost

DOBSON'S WELL, perhaps for *Tobar Dubh Sithean*. Well of the black little hill. *Tobar*, well; *dubh*, black, *sithean*, hillock.

DOD, DOD HILL, DOD LAW. All these words have the same meaning. Dod is a corruption of *cnoc*, hill, and law is *lamh*, hill.

DODRIDGE. Slope of the hill. *Ruigh*, slope; *cnoc*, hill. See Dod.

DOG. The island called the Lamb is between two islets which are called North Dog and South Dog, because they seem to be guarding the Lamb, but Lamb really means hill See Lamb.

DOGBUSH KNOWE. Knoll of the black bushy place. *Dubh*, black. Bh had become gh, and h had been lost.

DOLPHINGSTON. Black hill town *Doille*, darkness, dark; *fin*, hill. S represents in of fin.

DONOLLY. Hill at a turn or bend. *Dun*, hill; *uileann*, corner. If the pasture on a hill is very good olly may represent *olla*, productive of wool

DOON HILL. Hill. *Dun*, hill. The second part of the name is a translation of the first.

DOVE ROCK. Black rock. *Dubh* (bh equal to v), black.

DOW CRAIG. Black rock. *Dubh*, black. Bh is equal to u, v, or w.

DREM. Long hill. *Druim*, ridge.

DROWINHOWLET, for *Leth Droighneach Choill*. Side of the thorny hill. *Leth* (h silent), side; *droighneach* (gh and ch silent), thorny; *choill, coill* aspirated, hill. C is silent and oi became ow.

DRUM. Ridge of a long hill. *Druim*, ridge.

DRUMMORE. Big long hill. *Druim*, ridge; *mor*, big.

DRYDEN. Den of thorns *Dein*, den; *draigh*, thorn-tree

DRYLAW HILL. Hill where hawthorns grew. *Draigh*, thorn; *lamh*, hill.

DUDDY BURN. Dark burn. *Dubhach*, dark.

DUMBADAM. Brae of the hill. *Aodann*, brae; *dun*, hill. B is a euphonic addition to n changed to m.

DUNBAR. Point of the hill. *Barr*, point; *dun*, hill.

DUNCANLAW, DUNCAN'S PLANTATION, DUNCANSON'S WOOD. Duncan was originally *chuitail, cuitail* aspirated, fold, which became whitehill, and this was made in Gaelic *duncan*, white hill (*dun*, hill; *can*, white). Law is *lamh*, hill; son is *sithean* (th silent), hill. An of *can* and ean of *sithean* were regarded as plural terminations and made s, which was added to an and ean to make English possessives.

DUNCRA. Hill of the fold. *Dun*, hill; *cra*, wattled fold.

DUNCUR. Hill of the pool. *Dun*, hill; *curr*, pool.

DUNGLASS. Green hill. *Dun*, hill; *glas* (Irish), green.

DUNSIDE. Place on a hill. *Dun*, hill; *suidhe*, place, site.

DUNSTANE, for *Dun Sithean*, both parts of which mean hill. *Sithean* had become first stean and then stane.

DYE WATER Black water. *Dubh*, black. Bh, which is sometimes equal to y, had been changed to dh, always equal to y, and afterwards ye had been substituted for dh.

EACHIL RIG. Slope of the fold. *Ruigh*, slope; *chuitail, cuitail* aspirated, fold. *Chuitail* became whitehill, which was turned into Gaelic by *aodgeal*, white hill (*aod*, hill, *geal*, white). *Aodgeal* became in other names adziel, aigle, eagle, eccle, edge-hill, edzell.

EAGLESCARNIR. Fold on a little hill. For Eagle see Eachil Rig. Carnie is *carnan*, little hill, with an normally made ie It had been added to eagle to explain it in the belief that it meant hill. S was inserted to make eagle possessive and to connect it with carnie.

EAST RIG. East Slope. *Ruigh*, slope. The place of the name on the map shows that rig had been supposed to mean ridge.

EDINKENS BRIDGE. Bridge at a fold. The original form of Edinkens had been *chuitail, cuitail* aspirated, fold, which had been corrupted into whitehill. This was turned into Gaelic by *aodanncan*, white hill (*aodann*, hill, brae ; *can*, white) *Aodann* is now edin, and *can* is ken with s added because it ended in an, erroneously supposed to be a plural termination. It served to produce a possessive and to connect Edinken with Bridge *Aodann* is pronounced ed-an.

EEL BURN   Burn where eels are trapped on their way to the sea in autumn

ELDBOTLE. Beautiful house on a hill. *Ailde*, beauty, beautiful; *both*, house , *aill*, hill.

ELLY CLEUGH. Cleugh of the hill. *Aill*, hill

ELMSCLEUGH, for *Lamhan Cleugh*   Ravine in a hill *Lamhan*, diminutive of *lamh*, hill. *Lamhan* had been mistaken for *leamhan*, elm-tree.

ELPHINGSTONE. Town on a hill. *Aill*, hill , *fin*, hill.   S represents in of *fin*, supposed to be a plural termination. *Aill* had been prefixed to *fin* as an explanation.

ELSIE CLEUGH. Ravine of the hill. *Aill*, hill ; *sith* (th silent), hill

ELVINGSTON, for *Baile Aill Bheinn*. Town on a hill   *Baile*, town , *aill*, hill; *bheinn, beinn* aspirated, hill   *Aill* is a late addition made to explain ving, the corruption of *bheinn*.

EWEFORD. Ford at a fold. *Chuith, cuith* aspirated, fold. *Chuith* lost both the aspirated letters, and ui became ewe

EWELAIRS. Land at a fold. *Chuith, cuith* aspirated, fold ; *lar*, land. *Chuith* lost both its aspirated letters, and ui became ewe. Probably s had been added to lair in the belief that the name meant lying places for ewes.

EWELY WOOD. Wood of the fold on the hill   *Chuith, cuith* aspirated, fold , *lamh*, hill. Ch and th and mh had all been lost.

EWINGSTON. Town of the small fold. *Chuithan, cuithan* aspirated, small fold. Ch and th had both been lost, and an had become ing   Other forms of Ewing are Ewan and Ewen

EYE WATER. Water of the fold   *Chuith, cuith* aspirated, fold. Ch and th became silent and were lost

EYEBROUGHY, for *Chuith Bruchan*. Fold of the little hill. *Chuith, cuith* aspirated, fold , *bruchan*, small hill. *Chuith* lost ch with its vowel and also th, leaving i. An of *bruchan* normally became y.

FAIRNLY. Hill of cultivated land. *Lamh*, hill ; *farran* (Irish), land.

FALL   Fold   *Fal*, circle, fold.

FALSIDE. Site of a fold. *Suidhe*, place , *fal*, fold.

FASENY WATER. Burn passing a green place near a hill *Fatha* (tha silent), green place ; *sithean* (th silent), little hill An in *sithean* had normally become y, which should have taken the place of an instead of being added to it. The name is greatly corrupted, but its position on the Ordnance Survey map suggests the etymology given.

FAUSLY Fold side. *Fal*, fold ; *leth* (th silent), side. L is a movable letter, sometimes inserted where it ought not to be, and sometimes omitted where it ought to be.

FAWN KNOWES. Knoll on a gentle slope *Cnocan*, diminutive of *cnoc*, hill ; *fan*, gentle slope. An was improperly made es instead of ie.

FAWN WOOD. Wood on a gentle slope. *Fan*, gentle slope.

FEE CLEUGH. Ravine of the fold *Chuith, cuith* aspirated, fold. Ch became ph equal to f, and th, being silent, was lost. The fold was the large rectangular enclosure on the north side of the cleugh.

FEN BURN Hill burn. *Fin*, hill.

FENNIE LAW. Little hill. *Finan*, little hill ; *lamh*, hill. In Haddington i of fin is made e, as in Hen Moss, Henmuir, Fen Burn, Fenton.

FENTON. Hill town. *Fin*, hill.

FENTON BARNS. Farm office houses at Fenton.

FIDRA, for *Chuid Rath*. Fold. *Chuid, cuid* aspirated, fold ; *rath*, fold, circle. Ch became ph, equal to f ; and th being silent had been lost Fidra had once been pasture ground for cattle. The second part had been added to explain the first.

FIDRA BRIGS. Gaps in rocks between the mainland and Fidra island, through which the tide rushed with great force when rising or falling. *Bruchd*, rushing water.

FLACKYPARK. Windy park (400 feet above sea). *Flaicheach*, windy, stormy.

FLAT KILNS, for *Flath Coillean*. Knoll of the court. *Flatha*, court ; *coillean*, little hill. Barony courts had been held on the knoll.

FLUKE DUB. Wet muddy place. *Fliuch*, wet.

FOSTER LAW. Hill beside a hollow on a shieling. *Lamh*, hill ; *chos, cos* aspirated, hollow ; *airidh*, shieling. Mh is equal to w, bh had become ph, equal to f.

FORTH BRAE. Brae of the fold. *Chorth, corth* aspirated, fold. Ch became ph, which is f.

FORTON. Small fold. *Chortan, cortan* aspirated, small fold. Ch became ph, equal to f.

FOUL STEPS. Stepping stones at a pool. *Pholl, poll* aspirated, pool, burn. Ph is equal to f.

FOULSTRUTHER. Burn of the shieling. *Pholl, poll* aspirated, burn, pool , *sruth*, burn ; *airidh*, shieling Ph is equal to f. The first part is a late addition.

FOUNTAINHALL. Hill of the fountain. *Choill, coill* aspirated, hill.

FRIAR DYKES. Black hill. *Triath*, hill ; *dubh*, black.

FRIARS' CROOK. Hill. *Triath*, hill ; *cnoc*, hill. *Cnoc* is in some places pronounced crochg. Here crook may mean bend, as in English.

FRIARS' NOSE. Point of the hill. *Ness*, point, nose; *triath*, hill.

FRIZZELS' WOOD. Forest on a hill. *Frith*, forest, deer forest; *aill*, hill.

FULLERS HILL. Hill of the pool on the shieling *Pholl*, *poll* aspirated, pool; *airidh*, shieling Ph is equal to f. S made fuller possessive.

GAIRY BURN. Rough burn. *Gairbhe*, roughness, rough. Bh is equal to u, v, w, and sometimes it has become y in Scotch, as in Garry

GALLA LAW. Hill of the fold. *Chuitail*, *cuitail* aspirated, fold. *Chuitail* became whitehill, which was turned into Gaelic by *gealuchlamh*, white hill (*gealach*, white, *lamh*, hill), now become Galla Law.

GALLERY KNOWE. Knoll of the fold *Chuitail*, *cuitail* aspirated, fold *Chuitail* was corrupted into whitehill, which was turned into *gealruigh*, white hill, (*geal*, white, *ruigh*, slope of a hill). The personal name Gilroy is derived from *gealruigh*.

GALLOWS LAW Hill on which criminals convicted at Barony Courts were hanged. *Lamh*, hill.

GAMELSHIEL Hut at a fold on a hill. *Gamh*, primitive of *gamhann*, fold; *aill*, hill; *seal*, shiel, house on a shieling.

GAMUELSTON. Fold on the brow of a hillock. *Gamhann*, fold, *muilean*, brow of a hillock. Am had become ie and had been lost. S represents ean.

GARLETON Town on the rough side of a hill *Garbh*, rough; *leth*, side. Both bh and th had been dropped.

GARLICK ROCK. Rough flat stone *Garbh*, rough; *leac*, flat stone. Wild garlic grows in cliffs, and it may be referred to in the name.

GARVALD Rough burn. *Garbh* (bh equal to v), rough; *allt*, burn.

GATEFOOT. Windy fold. *Gaothach*, windy; *chuit*, *cuit* aspirated, fold. Ch became ph, equal to f

GATESIDE. Windy place. *Gaothach*, windy; *suidhe*, place.

GAVIN'S LEE. Grassy place at a fold. *Gabhann*, fold. Ann became s, improperly.

GEGAN. Small eminence. *Gigean*, something small.

GIANT HILL, for *Sithean* Hill. *Sithean* (th silent), small hill. Euphonic t had been added to n

GIBB'S HILL Fir hill. *Giubhas*, fir.

GIFFORD. Ford at a fold *Chuith*, *cuith* aspirated, fold. C became g, and th became ph, equal to f.

GILCHRISTON, for *Baile Chuit Crois*. Town at a fold where a burn was crossed. *Baile*, town, translated and put last; *chuit*, *cuit* aspirated, fold; *crois*, crossing. *Chuit* became white, and this was afterwards turned into Gaelic by *geal*, white *Geal* seems to qualify *crois*, therefore it was made *chrois* as following its adjective *Geal-chrois* Town is now Gilchriston.

GILDSWELL, for *Tobar Chuit*. Well at a fold. *Tobar*, well;

chuit, *cuit* aspirated, fold. *Chuit* became white, which was turned into Gaelic by *geal*, white, with euphonic d added to l.

GILMERTON, for *Baile Chuit Mor*. Town at the big fold. *Baile*, town; *chuit*, *cuit* aspirated, fold; *mor*, big, *Chuit* was corrupted into white, and subsequently it was turned into Gaelic by *geal*, white, now made gil.

GIN HEAD. Both parts mean fold. *Gamhann* (mh silent), fold; *chuid*, *cuid* aspirated, fold. C in *chuid* had been lost, being silent.

GLADSHOT. Place in a little howe. *Claiseag*, diminutive of *clais*, trench-like hollow.

GLADSMUIR. Muir frequented by kites. Glede (English), kite, glider.

GLEGHORNIE. Fold. Originally *Chuitail*, *cuitail* aspirated, fold, which became whitehill. This was afterwards turned into Gaelic by *gealcharnan*, white hill (*geal*, white; *charnan*, *carnan* aspirated, little hill). C in *charnan* being silent was lost, and an became ie, and *gealcharnan* is now Gleghornie.

GOES LAW. Hill of the fold. *Lamh*, hill; *gobhann*, fold. Bh, being silent, was lost. Ann was erroneously supposed to be a plural termination and was made es.

GOLD KNOWE. Hill. *Coill*, hill.

GOLET'S WELL, for *Tobar Gogh Leathan*. Well of the broad fold. *Tobar*, well; *gogh*, *gog*, with final g aspirated and silent, fold; *leathan*, broad. An had become s, improperly.

GOSFORD. Ford at a fir. *Giuthas* (th silent), fir.

GOSHEN, for *Gobha a Sithean*. Fold at a small hill. *Gobha*, fold; *sithean*, small hill. The aspirated letters and following vowels had been lost. Si is pronounced she, and go-shian had become Goshen.

GOSS BANK. Bank of the fold. *Gothann*, fold. Bh had become silent, and ann had wrongly been made s instead of ie. Bank might represent *chuid*, *cuid* aspirated, fold, corrupted into white, which was turned into Gaelic by *ban*, white, with euphonic k added.

GOURLYBANK. Bank on a hill where goats fed. *Gobhar*, goat, *lamh* (mh silent), hill.

GOWDIE'S WELL. Well at a small fold. *Cuidan*, small fold. C became g, and an normally became ie, and, abnormally, s also.

GOWKS CLEUGH. Ravine of the hill. *Cnoc*, hill. Gowk is a corruption of *cnoc* Perhaps s represents an of *cnocan*, diminutive of *cnoc*

GOWKS HILL. Hill. *Cnoc*, hill. Gowk is a corruption of *cnoc*.

GOWL BURN. Burn from a ridge where two slopes meet. *Gobhal*, ridge of a house.

GRANGEMUIR. Moor of the barn on a farm belonging to a religious convent ', Granea, (Latin), barn.

GRANTS BRAES. Sandy braes. *Grainneach* (Irish), sandy.

GRAY'S GOAT, for *Creagan Cuit*. Rock of the fold. *Creagan*, diminutive of *creag*, rock; *cuit*, fold

GRAY'S GOATS, for *Creagan Chuitan.* Rock of the small fold *Creagan,* diminutive of *creag,* rock, *cuitan,* diminutive of *cuit,* fold. An normally became s.

GREENHEAD. Green fold. *Chuid, cuid* aspirated, fold. C in ch was lost, and huid became head.

GREIG'S WALLS. Little town on a small hill. *Bailean,* small town; *creagan,* small hill. *Bailean* had been put last and aspirated, and ean had been made s improperly. Bh is equal to w, and bhails had been pronounced walls An of *creagan* had been made s instead of ie. Greig is a corruption of *creag,* hill, from which comes also the name Gray or Grey.

GRIPES. Turnings *Creapan,* plural of *creap* (Irish), turn, bend.

GULLANE Fold. *Gamhlann,* fold Mh is equal to ou.

GULLION'S CLEUGH. Cleugh in the shoulder of a hill. *Gualann,* shoulder, projection from the side of a hill.

HADDINGTON Town at a small fold. *Chuidan, cuidan* aspirated, small fold C in ch was lost.

HAILES. Little hill. *Choillean,* little hill. C is silent, and an had been made s instead of ie.

HAIRY CRAIG. Shieling hill. *Airidh,* shieling; *creag,* hill.

HALFLAND BARNS. Halfland is for *Chabh Lamhan.* Hollow between two hills *Chabh, cabh* aspirated, hollow; *lamhan,* plural of *lamh,* hill. C of *chabh* had been lost, l is a euphonic insertion, not usually sounded; bh had become ph or f; mh had been lost, being silent; and euphonic d had been added to an. Barns is *bearnas,* gap, added to explain half.

HALFMOON, for *Chabh Moine.* Hollow of the moor. *Chabh, cabh* aspirated, hollow, *moine,* moor. C of ch had been lost, and l had been introduced to obtain an English word. Bh had become ph, which is f.

HALL BURN. Hill burn. *Choill, coill* aspirated, hill. C had been lost

HALL EDGE. Brae of the hill. *Aod,* brae, *choill, coill* aspirated, hill

HALLOW CRAIG. Bare barren hill. *Fhalamh, falamh* aspirated, poor, unproductive; *creag,* hill. F in fh is silent and had been lost.

HALLS. Little hill. *Choillean, coillean* aspirated, hillock. C silent had been lost, and ean had improperly been changed to s

HANGING CRAIG, HANGING ROCKS Hanging is *fhangan, fangan* aspirated, little fold Craig is *creag,* hill. F in fh is silent.

HARE CLEUGH, HARE CRAIGS, HARE HEAD, HAREHOPE, HARE LAW, HARELAW, HARESHAW KNOWE, HARESTANES, HARESTONE HILL. Hare is *airidh,* shieling. Dh is silent and had been lost with the preceding vowel H had been prefixed for euphony and to obtain an English word. Head is *chuid, cuid* aspirated, fold, from which c had been dropped Hope is *chop, cop* aspirated,

c

hill, with silent c dropped. Law is *lamh*, hill. Knowe is *cnocan*, diminutive of *cnoc*, hill, with an made e.

HARLEY GRAIN. Branch of a burn coming from a shieling on a hill. Grain (Scotch), branch of a burn, *airidh*, shieling, *lamh*, hill.

HARP LAW. Hill of the shieling. *Lamh*, hill; *airidh*, shieling. Dh had become ph, and h had been dropped. H had been prefixed for euphony.

HARPERDEAN. Den of the shieling. *Dein*, den; *airidh*, shieling. H had been prefixed to *airidh* for euphony; and dh had been made ph, which afterwards lost h. Er is a repetition of *airidh* because it had been lost sight of in Harp.

HARRY'S BURN. Burn of the shieling. *Airidh*, shieling. Euphonic h had been prefixed to a.

HARTSIDE, for *Suidhe Ard*. Place on a hill. *Suidhe*, place; *ard*, hill.

HATTLE ROCKS. Rocks at a fold. *Chuitail*, *cuitail* aspirated, fold. C in ch is silent and had been lost.

HAYSTALL. Steep place at a fold. *Stalla*, steep bank, precipice; *chuith*, *cuith* aspirated, fold. C and th were lost, being silent, and hui became ay.

HAZELLY BURN. Burn of the fold. *Chuithail*, *cuithail* aspirated, fold. C in ch was lost, and z took the place of th.

HAZELLY CLEUGH. See Hazelly Burn.

HEART LAW. Hill of the shieling. *Lamh*, hill; *airidh*, shieling.

HEDDERWICK SANDS. Sands between two bays. *Eadar*, between; *uig*, nook, bay.

HENMUIR. Hill muir. *Fhin*, *fin* aspirated, hill. F, being silent, had been lost.

HERDMANSTON, for *Baile Airidh Man*. Town on a shieling on a hill. *Baile*, town; *airidh*, shieling; *man*, hill. H had been prefixed to *airidh* for euphony, and an of *man* had improperly been made s though *man* remained.

HERD'S HILL. Hill of the shieling. *Airidh*, shieling.

HERIOT BURN. Burn of the shieling. *Airidh*, shieling. H had been prefixed for euphony.

HERRING ROAD. Road to the shielings. *Airidhean*, plural of *airidh*, shieling; with euphonic h prefixed.

HIGHFIELD. Field of the fold. *Chuith*, *cuith* aspirated, fold. C and th, being silent, were lost.

HIGHLEE. Grassy place at a fold. Ley (Scotch), grass-land; *chuith*, *cuith* aspirated, fold. C had been lost, and th had become gh.

HIGHSIDE. Place at a fold. *Suidhe*, place; *chuith*, *cuith* aspirated, fold. C had been lost, and th had become gh.

HILLDOWN, for *Aill Dun*. Hill. *Aill*, hill; *dun*, hill. Hilldown has also the form Eildon.

HIRSTON LAW. Town in a wood on a hill. Hurst (Old English), wood; *lamh*, hill.

HODGES, perhaps for *Chuidan*. Small fold. *Chuidan, cuidan* aspirated, small fold. C had been lost, d had been pronounced as dg, and an had wrongly been made es instead of ie.

HOG RIG. Small slope   *Og*, small; *ruigh*, slope on a hill, shieling.

HOLLANDSIDE   Place on a little hill   *Suidhe*, place; *choillean, coillean* aspirated, little hill. C had been lost, and euphonic d had been added to n.

HOLYNBANK   If this name is of Gaelic origin Holyn represents *Choillean, coillean* aspirated, little hill. If it is of English origin it represents holin, holly.

HOOKSTER LAW. Breast of a cliff on a hill.   *Uchd*, breast; *stor*, cliff; *lamh*, hill.

HOOLY PATH. Birch hill.   *Beath*, birch, *choille, coille* aspirated, hill. C silent was lost.

HOPE HILLS. Probably the original name had been *Chop, cop* aspirated, hill, and when c silent had been lost *coillean*, little hill, had been added to explain it   Then *coillean* had been mistaken for the plural of *coill* and had been translated into hills

HOPE WATER. Burn from a hill   *Chop, cop* aspirated, hill.

HOPEFIELD. Hill field. *Chop, cop* aspirated, hill. *Chop* lost c and became hope.

HOPES. Little hill. *Chopan, copan* aspirated, little hill. C had been lost, and an had improperly been made es instead of ie.

HOPRIG, for *Ruigh Chop*. Slope of the hill. *Ruigh*, slope; *chop, cop* aspirated, hill.

HORNSHIEL   Hill. *Charn, carn* aspirated, hill. C had been lost, and a became o. S converted horn into a possessive.

HORSE LAW, for *Thorran Lamh*. Hill. *Thorran, torran* aspirated, little hill, *lamh*, hill   T, being silent, had been lost, and an had become s instead of ie   N of *cnoc* became r, a common occurrence.

HORSECROOK, for *Torran Cnoc*. Hill. *Thorran, torran* aspirated, little hill; *cnoc*, hill. T, being silent, had been lost, and an had been made s instead of ie   N of *cnoc* became r, a common occurrence.

HOWDEN. Little fold   *Chuidan, cuidan* aspirated, little fold C silent was lost.

HOWDENFLAT, for *Chuidan Flaith*. Little fold for milking *Chuidan, cuidan* aspirated, fold, *flaith*, milk.

HUMBIE. Small hill. *Thoman, toman* aspirated, little hill. T in *thoman* is silent, b had been added to m for euphony, and an normally became ie

HUMMELL. Both parts mean hill. *Thom, tom* aspirated, hill; *meall*, hill. T in *thom*, being silent, had been lost.

HUNGRY SNOUT   Projecting rock on a shieling hill. *Fhin, fin* aspirated, hil, *airidh*, shieling. F, being silent, had been lost, and i became n

HUNTINGDON. Hill of assembly *Dun*, hill; *choinne, coinne* aspirated, assembly. C was lost, and t was added to n.

HUNTLAW. Hill of assembly. *Lamh*, hill; *choinne, coinne* aspirated, assembly. C had been lost, and euphonic t had been added to n.

HURKLETILHIM. Pool or well on a hill. Hurkle is for *Churr Coill.* Well or pool on a hill. *Churr, curr* aspirated, place where there is water; *coill,* hill. Tilhim is *tholm, tolm* aspirated, hill, added to explain *coill* after it had been corrupted.

ICE CLEUGH. Ravine of the burn. *Eas*, burn.

INCH. Enclosed place. *Innis*, enclosure. The Inch is a place where drovers had a right to fold cattle at night.

INGLISFIELD. Field of the little fold. *An Chuitan*, the little fold. *An*, the; *chuitan, cuitan* aspirated, little fold. *Chuitan* became whitean, which was afterwards turned into Gaelic by *gealan*, diminutive of *geal*, white. An became s instead of ie, and *an gealan* is now Inglis. Gilzean and Giles are other derivatives from *gealan*.

INKS, originally *Chuitail*, fold. *Chuitail* became whitehill, which was turned into Gaelic by *fhincan*, white hill (*fhin, fin* aspirated, hill; *can*, white). Fh silent was lost, an was improperly made s, leaving incs, now Inks. Seven places on the estuary of the Peffer burn are called Inks

INNER HILL. Hill of the shieling. *Fhin, fin* aspirated, hill; *airidh*, shieling. Fh had been lost, being silent.

INNERWICK. Nook at the hill of the shieling. *Uig*, nook, *fhin, fin* aspirated, hill; *airidh*, shieling.

JAG. Good place. *Deagh*, ground.

JAMIE'S NEUK. Corner where sheep were shorn. *Deamhsadh*, fleecing, shearing.

JANEFIELD, for *Achadh Sean*. Old place. *Achadh*, place, *sean* (pronounced shean), old.

JINKIE BURN. Burn of the fold. *Chuitail, cuitail* aspirated, fold. *Chuitail* became whitehill, made in Gaelic *dun-can*, white hill, *dun* (pronounced dgun), hill; *can*, white. An became ie.

JOHNSCLEUGH. Cleugh on a hill. *Dun* (pronounced dgun), hill.

JOHNSTONE'S HOLE. Johnston represents *Dun Sithean*, hill. *Dun*, hill; *sithean*, hill. Ean had been made s. Hole is a deep place near the edge of the sea.

JOPHIES NEUK. Nook of the black little fold. *Dubh*, black; *chuithan, cuithan* aspirated, little fold. J in names often represents d. Ch of *chuithan* had become ph, and th, being silent, had been lost. An had normally become ie, but it had also been made s, abnormally, and both ie and s had been used instead of an.

JULIA CROWN. Black round hillock. *Doille*, darkness, dark; *cruinn*, round place.

KAE HEUGH. Cliff in which jackdaws build. *Cathag* (th silent), jackdaw. The sound of the name resembles the voice of the bird, as jack does in the English name

KAMEHILL Hill rising to a sharp ridge Kaim (Scotch), comb, crest of a cock

KEITH. Fold *Cuith*, fold.

KELL BURN. Narrow burn. *Caol*, narrow.

KEMPLE BANK. Level terrace above a crooked burn. *Cam*, crooked, *poll*, pool, burn.

KER LAW. Hill. *Cathair* (th silent), hill; *lamh*, hill

KIDLAW. Hill of the fold. *Cuid*, fold, *lamh*, hill.

KILLDUFF Black head *Cinn*, second form of *ceann*, head; *dubh*, black. *Cinn* had been made cill, now kill. Bh had become ph, equal to f, which had been doubled unnecessarily

KILLPALLET. Head of a protected fold. *Cinn*, second form of *ceann*, head; *peallte*, past participle of *peall*, to protect.

KILMADE BURN Burn at the head of a level piece of ground, *Cinn*, head, *madh*, variant of *magh*, plain. *Cinn* had become cill.

KILMURDIE, for *Cinn Mur Dubh*. Head of the black hill. *Cinn*, second form of *ceann*, head; *mur*, hill, *dubh*, black. Bh of *dubh* had become gh, equal to y.

KILRIG. Head of the slope. *Cinn*, second form of *ceann*, head; *ruigh*, slope.

KINCHIE. Head of the fold *Cinn*, second form of *ceann*, head; *chuith*, *cuith* aspirated, fold. U and th had been lost, being silent.

KINGSIDE. Head of the place. *Cinn*, second form of *ceann*, head; *suidhe*, place

KINGSIDE RIG Ridge of the head of the place *Ruigh*, slope, here supposed to mean ridge; *cinn*, second form of *ceann*, head; *suidhe*, place. The place indicated is an ancient fold divided internally into four parts.

KINGSLAW Head of the hill *Ceann*, head; *lamh*, hill S represents ann in *ceann*

KINGSTON. Town on the head of a hill *Cinn* for *ceann*, head.

KIPPIELAW. Hill. *Ceapan*, little hill, *lamh*, hill.

KIRK YARD SHOT. Small piece of ground adjoining the old churchyard of Ormiston *Sgot*, spot, detached part.

KIRKLAND, KIRKLANDHILL. The names mean hill. *Creag*, hill, *lamhan*, hill Mh, being silent, had been lost, and euphonic d had been added to an.

KITCAT STAIRS. Stairs on the way to a fold. *Cat*, road, way, *cuit*, fold

KNOCK, KNOCK HILL. Hill. *Cnoc*, hill.

KNOCKENHAIR. Little hill on a shieling *Cnocan*, little hill; *airidh*, shieling. *Airidh* lost idh

KNOWES, KNOLL. *Cnocan*, little hill An by mistake became es instead of ie. *Cnocan* had become cnollan, and when ll was lost o became ow, as in pow for poll, bow for boll, row for roll.

LADY'S WOOD. Broad wood *Leathan,* broad. Th had become dh, and an had abnormally become s. Dh is equal to y.

LAIRD'S GARDEN. Lairds is for *Liath Ardan.* Grey little hill. *Liath* (th silent), grey ; *ardan,* little hill, with an made s instead of ie. Garden is for *Garbh Dun,* rough hill *Garbh,* rough ; *dun,* hill.

LAMB HILL. Hill. *Lamh,* hill

LAMBLAIR. Hill land. *Lamh,* hill ; *lair,* second form of *lar,* land. Euphonic b had been added to m.

LAMMER LAW. Hill of the shieling. *Lamh,* hill ; *airidh,* shieling ; *lamh,* hill. The last part is a late addition.

LAMPLAND, for *Lamh Lamhan.* Hill. *Lamh,* hill, with euphonic p ; *lamhan,* small hill, with euphonic d. H in *lamh* and mha in *lamhan* had been lost.

LAMPOCK. Small hill. *Lamh,* hill ; *og,* small.

LANDRIDGE. Slope. *Ruigh,* slope ; *lamhan,* hill. Euphonic d had been added to an.

LATCH. Wet place in a hollow crossing a road. *Lathach,* mire, muddy place.

LAVEROCKLAW, for *Lamh Ruigh Lamh.* Slope of the hill. *Lamh,* hill ; *ruigh,* slope ; *lamh,* hill. The first *lamh* is a late addition.

LAW KNOWES, for *Lamhan.* Little hill. An had been regarded as a plural termination, and hence s had been added to knowe.

LAW ROCK. The name had originally been *Creag,* rock, but *creag* also means hill, and *lamh,* hill, had been prefixed as an explanation.

LAWEND Small hill. *Lamhan* (mh silent), little hill

LAWFIELD. Hill field. *Lamh,* hill.

LAWHEAD. Head of the hill. *Lamh,* hill.

LAWRIE'S DEN. Fox's Den The fox was formerly called Lowrie or Tod Lowrie because he lowered his ears when approaching his prey.

LEAP ROCKS. Rocks at a bend. *Luib,* bend, turn.

LECKANBANE. White rocks. *Leacan,* smooth rocks ; *ban,* white

LECKS. Smooth rocks. *Leacan,* plural of *leac,* smooth, flaggy rock.

LEEHOUSE. Stone at a fold. *Lia,* stone , *chuith, cuith* aspirated, fold. Ch lost c, and th became sh, and afterwards s.

LEEHOUSES. Stone at a small fold. *Lia,* stone ; *chuithan, cuithan* aspirated, little fold. C of ch was lost, th became sh and s by loss of the aspirate, and an became es improperly instead of ie.

LEITHIES. Broad rock. *Leathan,* broad. An became ie but some made it ı, both of which were added to the first part.

LENNOXLOVE, for *Lamh Leathan Uisge.* Hill of the broad water. *Lamh,* hill ; *leathan,* broad ; *uisge,* stream (Tyne).

LETHAM, for *Leathan*. Broad place. *Leathan*, broad

LETHINGTON. Broad hill. *Leathan*, broad; *dun*, hill.

LIMYLANDS, for *Liomhaidh Lamhan*. Smooth hill. *Liomhaidh*, smooth, *lamhan*, hill. An improperly became s, and euphonic d was added to an.

LING HOPE. Long hill. Ling (Scotch), long; *chop*, *cop* aspirated, hill This name has been misplaced on the Ordnance Survey Map. Instead of being put on a hill it has been put along a burn valley.

LING RIG. Long ridge, this seems to be the meaning assigned to the name on the Ordnance Survey Map, but Rig (for *ruigh*), means the slope near the base of a hill.

LINGHOPE STEEL Burn of the long hill. *Steall*, gushing spring, burn. The name has been placed on a hill instead of a burn.

LINKS. Sandy terraces near the sea. *Lianan*, plural of *lian*, plain, level, grass-land. Euphonic k had been inserted, and an had normally become s, producing lianks, now Links.

LINKYLEE. Small level grassy place. *Leanan*, diminutive of *lean*, plain, ley (Scotch), grass-land K, equal to c, had been added to *lean*, and an had normally become y. In links s represents an as a plural termination.

LINPLUM. Plunge at a waterfall. *Linne*, waterfall; *plumb*, noise made by falling water

LINT BURN Burn *Linne*, pool, burn, waterfall, with euphonic t added

LINTON. Town at a linn. *Linne*, linn, waterfall, pool.

LITTLE GAVEL. Small fold. *Gabhal*, fold.

LODGE RIG, for *Ruigh Leoid*. Slope of the side of a hill. *Ruigh*, slope; *leoid*, second form of *leud*, side. D had been sounded dg.

LONG CLEUGH. Ravine in a hill *Lamhan*, hill, made first lang and afterwards long, but the cleugh is not long.

LONG CRAIGS Long rocks. *Creagan*, plural of *creag*, rock.

LONG CRIB RIG. Ridge of the hill of the fold. *Ruigh*, slope, supposed to mean ridge, *lamhan*, hill; *crubh*, fold, fank. *Lamhan* had become lang, which is now Long.

LONG GRAIN. Hill branch of a burn. *Lamhan*, hill, corrupted into lang, and anglicised into Long. Grain is one of two or more branches of a burn.

LONG NEWTON. Newton on the hill. Long had been lang, which represents *lamhan*, hill Mh being equal to nasal v an had become ang.

LONG YESTER Hill of Yester. *Lamhan*, hill. Mh became silent and was dropped, but being equal to nasal v an became ang, now made ong See Yester.

LONGNIDDRY. Burn on the slope of a hill *Nid*, burn, *ruigh*, slope, *lamhan*, diminutive of *lamh*, hill *Lamhan* is a late addition made to explain *ruigh*.

LONGSKELLY. Long Rocks. *Sgeilg*, rock. In the form *sgeilgh* gh is equal to y.

LOTHIAN EDGE. Brae on the side of a hill. *Aod*, brae; *leothardean*, diminutive of *leothaid*, a secondary form of *leathad*, side. D in Gaelic is often sounded like dg. *Aod* had become Edge in several Scotch and English names.

LOWRANS LAW, for *Lamh Rathan Lamh*. Hill of the small fold *Lamh*, hill; *rathan* (th silent), small circle or fold; *lamh*, hill. The last *lamh* had been added to explain the first. An in *rathan* is a diminutive termination, not a plural, but s had been added to an by mistake.

LUFFNESS Wet point. *Fhliuch, fliuch* aspirated, wet; *ness*, point. Fh is usually silent and had been lost. Ch had become ph, equal to f, and f had been doubled unnecessarily. Much of the ground about Luffness House is less than twenty-five feet above sea level.

LUGGATE. Milking place. *Leigeadh*, milking.

LUTE LAW. Small law. *Luth*, small.

MACMERRY, for *Magh Murean*. Level high ground. *Magh*, plain; *murean*, diminutive of *mur*, hill. Ean normally became y

MADYAD, for *Madh Aod*. Level place on a hill. *Madh*, same as *magh*, plain; *aod*, brae, hill. Dh is equal to y.

MAGGIE'S¦ LOUP, for *Luib Maghan*. Bend in the little plain. *Luib*, bend; *maghan*, diminutive of *magh*, plain.

MAG'S BANK. Little level bank *Maghan*, diminutive of *magh*, plain. An had improperly been made s.

MAIDEN STONE. Middle of the hill. *Meadhon*, middle; *sithean*, hill. *Sithean* had become stane, and stane has become stone.

MAIDENS. Middle Rocks. *Meadhon*, middle. S in Maidens represents on, supposed to be a plural termination.

MAIDEN'S FOOT. Middle fold. *Meadhon*, middle; *chuit, cuit* aspirated, fold. Ch became ph, equal to f. S represents on, supposed to be a plural termination.

MAINS. Farm occupied by the landlord of an estate. Mains is a shortened form of domains, which comes through the French language from dominicalis (Latin), pertaining to a landlord.

MAINSHILL. Hill. *Man*, hill. S represents an in *man*, and hill is a translation of *man*.

MALCOLM'S LODGE. Malcolm represents *Maol Coillean*. Bare, smooth-topped little hill. *Maol*, bald; *coillean*, little hill.

MARION'S CLEUGH. Ravine on the side of a little hill. *Murean*, diminutive of *mur*, hill.

MARKLE. Big hill *Mor*, big; *choill, coill* aspirated, hill.

MARLION GRAIN. Marlion is probably a corruption of *Mur Lamhan*, both parts of which mean hill. *Mur*, hill; *lamhan*, diminutive of *lamh*, hill. Grain (English), means a branch of another burn.

MARLY KNOWE. Clay knoll Marl commonly means a mixture of clay and lime. Sometimes it means impure limestone, and sometimes clay.

MARVINGSTON. Town on a big hill. *Mor*, big; *bheinn, beinn* aspirated, hill. Bh is equal to v.

MAYSHIEL. Shiel in a plain. *Seal*, shiel, *magh*, plain.

MEAN CLEUGH. Small Cleugh. *Mean*, small

MEG'S BRIDGE. Big bridge. *Meug*, bulk, great.

MEIKLE SAYS LAW. Big upstanding hill Meikle (Scotch), big, *seas*, to stand up; *lamh*, hill

MEIKLERIG. Big slope. Meikle (Scotch), big, *ruigh*, slope.

MEL BURN Hill burn. *Meall*, hill.

MERRYFIELD. Little hill field. *Murean*, diminutive of *mur*, hill

MERRYHATTON. Little fold on a hillock. *Chuitan, cuitan* aspirated, little fold, *murean*, little hill Ean normally became y.

MERRYLAWS. Both parts mean small hill *Murean*, small hill; *lamhan*, small hill Ean became y normally, and an became s, abnormally.

MIDDLE NESS. Middle point between two burns *Ness*, point.

MILLER'S BENCH Bench on a shieling hill. *Mill*, second form of *meall*, hill, *airidh*, shieling Idh had been lost, being silent.

MILLSIT KNOWES. Knoll of sweetness *Millsead*, sweetness, *cnocan*, diminutive of *cnoc*, hill An had been made ie instead of s

MILSEY ROCKS. Rocks of sweetness. *Milse* (Irish), sweetness. The rocks had produced some plant sweet to taste, as dulse, or sweet to smell, as sea-pink *Milse* or *millse* is cognate with Latin *mel*, honey.

MITCHELLHALL, for *Choill Bheithach Aill* Hill of the birchy hill. *Choill, coill* aspirated, hill, *bheithach, beithach* aspirated, full of birches, *aill*, hill The last part of Mitchellhall is a recent addition to explain ell. Th had been strengthened by inserting c.

MOFFAT. Big fold. *Mo*, second form of *mor*, great; *chuit, cuit* aspirated, fold Ch became ph, equal to f.

MONKRIG, for *Ruigh Monadh* Slope of the hill. *Ruigh*, slope; *monadh*, hill, moor. Euphonic k had been added to n.

MONYNUT EDGE. Hill of the moor of the fold. *Aod*, hill, brae; *moine*, moor; *an*, of the; *chuit, cuit* aspirated, fold. *Aod*, is the primitive of *aodann*, brae. D is sounded as dg and *aod* has become Edge This name is given on the Ordnance Survey map to a high ridge four miles long Probably it had originally been applied to a small part at the south-east end of the ridge

MORHAM. Big dwelling-place *Mor*, big, ham (Frisian), dwelling.

MOULD BRIDGE. Bridge at a little hill *Mulan*, hillock D had sometimes been added to *mulan* for euphony, and it reappears in Mould.

MOUNT, for *Monadh*, moor.

. MOUNTLEHOY. The original name had been *Tulach Chuith.* Hill of the fold. *Tulach,* hill; *chuith, cuith* aspirated, fold. To this had been prefixed *monadh,* hill, to explain *tulach* after it had been corrupted.

MUNGOSWELLS, for *Bhailean Moine Chuith.* Little town on the moor of the fold. *Bhailean, bailean* aspirated, little town; *moine,* moor; *chuith,* fold. *Bailean* had been aspirated and put last, and ean had improperly been made s. Bh is equal to w, and wails became wells. Final th is silent, and *cuith* had become go, though it is usually made gow, as in Glasgow. S turned Mungo into the possessive.

MURRAYS, for *Mur Abhainn.* Hill of the stream. *Mur,* hill; *abhainn,* stream. *Ainn* being regarded as a plural termination, s had been substituted for inn.

MUTTON HOLE. Middle Hill. *Meadhon,* middle; *choill, coill* aspirated, hill.

MYLES, MYLDS, MULAN, hillock, with an abnormally made s. Euphonic d had sometimes been added to an, which appears in Mylds.

NEEDLE CLEUGH. Ravine of the burn of the hill. Cleugh (Scotch), ravine; *ned,* burn; *aill,* hill.

NEEDLESS. Burn at a fold. *Ned,* burn; *lios* (o silent), fold.

NETTLES CLEUGH. Ravine of the burn passing a fold. *Net,* burn, *lios,* fold.

NEWBYTH, for *An Chuith Beathach.* The fold in a birchy place. *An,* the; *chuith, cuith* aspirated, fold; *beathach,* place of birches. *An* had lost a, *chuith* had lost both ch and th, and *beathach* had lost ach.

NEWHALL, for *An Chuith Choill.* The fold of the hill. Originally the name had been *Coill an Chuith.* Hill of the fold. *An,* the; *chuith, cuith* aspirated, fold; *choill, coill* aspirated, hill. *An* lost a, *chuith* lost ch and th, *choill* lost c, and *hoill* became hall.

NEWLANDS, NEWLANDS HILL, for *An Chuith Lamhan.* The fold on the hill. Originally the name had been *Lamhan an Chuith.* Hill of the fold. *An,* the; *chuith, cuith* aspirated, fold; *lamhan,* diminutive of *lamh,* hill. *An* lost a; *chuith* lost its aspirated letters; and *lamhan* lost mha. Euphonic d was added to an, and s was added to d because *lamhan* had erroneously been regarded as a plural instead of a diminutive word. There are large old folds near Newlands and Newlands Hill.

NEWTONLEES. New town at a fold. *Lios,* fold.

NICHOLSON'S WELL, for *Tobar an Choill Sithean.* Well of the hill. *Tobar,* well; *an,* of the; *choill, coill* aspirated, hill. *Sithean* (now made son), had been added at a late date to explain *choill* after being corrupted. Ean had been made s instead of ie

NINE STONE RIG. Slope on which there are nine stones in a circle round a prehistoric grave. *Ruigh,* slope of a hill. In some places it is equivalent to shieling.

NINEWAR, for *Barr Nithan*   Head of the little burn. *Barr,* head ; *nithan,* little burn. *Barr* had been aspirated and put last, making *Nithan Bharr,* in which tha is silent, and bh is equal to w.

NINEWELLS BURN, for *Bhaile Nigheachan* Burn. Burn passing a town where cloth was washed   *Bhaile, baile* aspirated, town , *nigheachan,* washing   Bh is equal to w, and *bhaile* had become waile, and afterwards wells, as being connected with the English word nine. The Gaelic words *nighean,* maiden, *nigheachan,* washing, and the English word nine. which are pronounced in the same way, are often used one for another in names

NIPPER KNOWES, for *Cnocan Chnap Airidh.* Knoll of the head of the shieling. *Cnocan,* diminutive of *cnoc,* hill ; *chnap, cnap* aspirated, head, summit ; *airidh,* shieling. *Cnocan* was erroneously believed to be plural and made Knowes. *Chnap* lost ch, and *airidh* lost idh, and *nap an* became Nipper. The personal name Napier is another derivative from *Chnap Airidh.*

NORTH BERWICK   Berwick is for *Bear Uig.* Sharp point at a nook   *Bear,* spit , *uig,* bay, cove.

OATFIELD. Field of the fold   *Chuit, cuit* aspirated, fold. Ch, having become silent, had been lost, and ui had been changed to oa to get an English word.

OGLE BURN. Small burn. *Oghail,* small.

OLDHAMSTOCKS, for *Stocan Alltan.* Fold formed of trunks of trees stuck into the ground near a little burn   *Stocan,* plural of *stoc,* trunk of a tree; *alltan,* small burn. An of *stocan* had normally become s.

OLIVER'S SHIP   Oliver may represent *Oilean Bhir.* Island of the spit. *Oilean,* island ; *bhir, bir* aspirated, sharp point. Ean had become ie, and bh had become v, producing olievir, now Oliver   Probably the original form of the name had been *Bir Oilean.* Spit of the island. Ship may be a corruption of spit.

ORMISTON   East fertile place   *Or,* east , *meas,* high renown for fertility.

OSWALD DEAN   Den with a burn having a town on it. *Dein,* den, dean ; *uisge,* water, burn ; *bhaile, baile* aspirated, town. Bh is equal to w and *bhaile* became wal. D is a common euphonic addition to l.

OX CLEUGH   Ravine of a burn. *Uisge,* water, burn.

OX CRAIGS. Rocks at the edge of the sea. *Uisge,* water.

OXROAD BAY. Bay at the breast of the slope   *Uchd,* breast, brow ; *ruigh,* slope. Gh and dh are pronounced in the same way, hence g and d are sometimes mistaken for one another

OXWELL MAINS. Farm with its town on a burn. Mains, farm town cultivated by the proprietor. See Mains. *Bhaile, baile* aspirated, town , *uisge,* water.

PADDY BURN   Burn flowing past a hill with a hump. *Pait,* hump.

PAINS LAW. Punishment hill. *Peanas,* punishment

PALMERTON, for *Baile Mor*. Big town. *Baile*, town ; *mor*, big.

PANWOODLEES, for *Beinn Bhad Lios*. Hill of the wood at a fold. *Beinn*, hill ; *bhad, bad* aspirated, wood ; *lios*, fold. *Bhad* had been pronounced wad, which had become wood. O in lios is silent, and *lios* is pronounced lees.

PAPANA WATER. Burn flowing through ground belonging to the Catholic Church. *Papanach*, Catholic, belonging to the Pope.

PAPPLE. Shaggy hill. *Papach*, rough, shaggy ; *aill*, hill.

PARTAN CLEUGH. Ravine of the mountain ash. *Partainn* (Irish), rowan-tree.

PARTAN CRAIG. Rock where crabs are found. *Partan*, crab.

PEARLSTANE, for *Pior Aill Sithean*. Small hill. *Pior*, small ; *aill*, hill ; *sithean*, little hill. *Sithean* lost i and h and became stean, now stane. *Sithean* is a late addition explaining *aill*.

PEASTON. Small town. *Pios*, small.

PEAT LAW. Hill of peats. *Foid*, peat. F is equal to ph, which by loss of the aspirate becomes p. It is unlikely that the Scotch word peat is of Anglo-Saxon origin, as in dictionaries it is said to be, and it is probably a derivative from *foid*.

PEFFER, for *Chuith Airidh*. Fold on a shieling. *Chuith, cuith* aspirated, fold ; *airidh*, shieling. Ch became ph and h was lost. Th became ph, equal to f, which was doubled unnecessarily. Idh of *airidh* was lost.

PENCAITLAND. The oldest part of the name is Pencait, hill of the fold. *Beinn*, hill ; *cuit*, fold. *Lamhan*, hill, had been added to explain pen. D is a euphonic addition to an.

PENCRAIG. Hill. *Beinn*, hill ; *creag*, hill.

PENDRACHIN. Hill of thorns. *Beinn*, hill , *draighionn*, thorn, hawthorn

PENS ROUNALL. Round group of trees on a hillock. *Beinnan*, diminutive of *beinn*, hill. B had become p, and an had improperly been made s.

PENSHIEL HILL. Hill of the shiel. *Beinn*, hill ; *seal*, shiel, temporary residence on summer pasture. In the south of Scotland *beinn* becomes pen, usually pronounced pan.

PENSTON, for *Baile Beinn*. Town on a hill. *Baile*, town ; *beinn*, hill. S represents einn, erroneously supposed to be an, a plural termination. The insertion of s is late.

PENTLE. Hill. *Beinn*, hill ; *tulach*, hill.

PEPPERCRAIG, for *Creag Chuith Airidh*. Hill of the fold on a shieling. *Creag*, hill ; *chuith, cuith* aspirated, fold , *airidh*, shieling. Ch became ph but h was lost. Th also became ph and h was lost.

PETERSMUIR. Muir of the hump. *Paitean*, diminutive of *pait*, hump. *Pait* had been regarded as identical with Pat or Peter, and ean had been made s, which was added to Peter.

PHANTASSIE, for *Fan t-Easan*. Gentle slope at a small burn. *Fan*, gentle slope ; t euphonic addition to n ; *easan*, diminutive of *eas*, burn. In the Highlands *eas* often means waterfall.

PHILIP BURN, PHILIPSBURN. Burn from a hill. *Coillean*, diminutive of *coille*, hill. By mistake *coillean* had been thought to be *cuilean*, whelp, which is now corrupted into Philp and Philip

PHILIPSTOWN. Town on a little hill. *Coillean*, little hill. *Coillean* lapsed into *cuilean*, whelp in English and folp in Scotch, from which came filp, now made Philp and Philip, but Philip is properly a derivative from a Greek word meaning fond of horses

PICKERSTONE HILL. Hill of the stone on the summit of the shieling. *Pic*, point; *airidh*, shieling

PICKLETILLHIM This name is a combination of words meaning hill. *Pic*, pointed hill; *aull*, hill; *tulach*, hill; *thom*, tom aspirated, hill T in *thom* is silent and had been lost.

PILMUIR. Pool on a moor. *Poll*, pool.

PIN COD Hill of the fold. *Beinn*, hill, *cuid*, fold.

PINKERTON, for *Baile Fin Airidh*. Town on the hill of the shieling. *Baile*, town; *fin*, hill; *airidh*, shieling. F is equal to ph and by loss of the aspirate *fin* became pin. Euphonic k had been added to pin, producing Pink

PINLY. Both parts mean hill. *Fin*, hill, *lamh*, hill F is equal to ph, and the aspirate had been lost Mh had been lost, and a became y

PIRMIRS CLEUGH Ravine eroded in a little hill *Piorr*, to erode, *murean*, diminutive of *mur*, hill. Ean had improperly been regarded as a plural termination, instead of a diminutive.

PIRNIE GAP *Bearna*, long hollow, gap.

PISHWANTON Little fold *Pios*, small; *chuitail*, cuitail aspirated, fold. *Chuitail* became whitehill, which was afterwards turned into Gaelic by *bhandun*, white hill (*bhan*, *ban* aspirated, white, *dun*, hill). Bh being equal to w *bhan* became wan

PITCOX. Place on a little hill. *Pit*, place, *cnocan*, little hill. An became s, improperly, which combining with c made x.

PLATTCOCK Windy hill. *Plathach*, windy, *cnoc*, hill.

PLATTCOCK END, for *Plathach Cnocan*, windy little hill. An became first en and next end.

PLEA WELL. Well at a milking-fold. *Bliochd* (ochd silent), milk

PLEASANTS Open space at a hill *Plae*, open place, high road; *sithean*, hill. Th and the contiguous vowels had been lost. T had been added to an for euphony, and an had been made s though not a plural termination here.

POINT GARRY. Rough point *Garbh*, rough.

POWSHIEL. Shiel at a pool *Seal*, shiel, temporary residence; *poll*, pool. When ll is dropped o becomes ow

PRESLY. Bushy hill. *Preas*, bush, *lamh*, hill.

PRESSMENNAN. Bushy little hill *Preas*, bush, *manan*, little hill.

PRESTONKIRK. Kirk in a town at a bushy place. *Preas*, bush.

PRESTONPANS. Pans for evaporating sea water in making salt at Preston. Preston, town at a wooded place. *Preas*, bush.

PRIEST BANK. Bushy bank. *Preas*, bush.

PRIEST CLEUGH. Bushy ravine. *Preas*, bush.

PRIEST LAW. Bushy hill. *Preas*, bush ; *lamh*, hill.

PRIEST'S PULPIT, for *Pit Preasach Poll*. Bushy place at a burn. *Pit*, place ; *preasach*, bushy ; *poll*, burn

PRIEST'S WARD. Enclosed place where bushes grow. *Preas*, bush.

PROVOST'S PARK. Park of the big fold. *Buaile*, fold ; *mor*, big *Buaile mor* had been supposed to be *Baillidh mor*, big bailie, provost

PUDDLE BURN. Burn of the fold. *Chuidail, cuidail* aspirated, fold. Ch became ph and h was lost.

QUARREL SAND. Sand quarry *Coireall*, quarry.

QUEBEC ROCKS. Rocks resembling a cheese. *Cabag*, cheese, kebbock.

QUEENSTON BANK, for *Chuit Baile Choinne*. Fold at a place where assemblies were held. *Chuit, cuit* aspirated, fold ; *baile*, town ; *choinne, coinne* aspirated, meeting, assembly. *Chuit* became white, which was made *ban*, white, with euphonic k added. In Scotch names *choinne* has become quheen, queen, and whing.

RAGSTONE RIG. Probably Rag and Rig both represent *Ruigh*, slope of a hill, and stone may have been *sithean*, little hill, made in succession stane, and stone.

RAMMER DOD. Hill of the fold. Rammer is for *Rath Mur*. Fold on a hill. *Rath* (th silent), fold ; *mur*, hill. Dod is a corruption of *cnoc*, hill, added to explain *mur* after it had been corrupted. See Dod.

RANGELY KIPP, for *Rathan Chuitail*. Fold. *Rathan* (th silent), fold ; *chuitail, cuitail* aspirated, fold. *Chuitail* became whitehill, and this was afterwards made in Gaelic *gealach ceap*, white hill ; (*gealach*, white ; *ceap*, hill). *Gealach* has become gely, and *ceap* is now kipp.

RATTLEBAGS QUARRY, for *Coireall Rath Tulach Baghach*. Quarry at the big fold on a round knoll *Coireall*, quarry ; *rath*, fold ; *tulach*, round little hill ; *baghach*, big. *Baghach* becomes also bauch, baggie, and bag. A thick heavy rope of straw on the eave of a house or a rick is called a bagrope or a baggierope.

RAVENS HEUGH, RAVENSHEUGH. Steep bank at the foot of a slope on a hill. *Ruigh*, slope ; *bheinn, beinn* aspirated, hill.

RED MAINS Farm cultivated by the proprietor of an estate, situated on high level ground *Reidh*, level. See Mains.

RED SCAR. Red upstanding rock on a hill *Sgor*, rock rising above a hill.

REDCOLL. Hill with a flat top. *Reidh*, level , *coill*, hill.

REDDEN GRAIN. Branch of a burn flowing in a red ravine. Red might represent *reidh*, level.

REDSIDE. Level place. *Reidh*, level ; *suidhe*, place.

REEN RIG, for *Ruighean Ruigh*. Slope. *Ruighean* (gh silent), small slope ; *ruigh*, slope   The second part explained the first

REIDS' HILL, REIDSHILL. Hill with a level summit. *Reidh*, level plain

RENTONHALL. Town at the point of a hill. *Rann*, point ; *choill, coill* aspirated, hill   In *choill* c was lost, and oi became a.

RHODES, for *Ruighean*. Little slope. *Ruighean*, diminutive of *ruigh*, slope. Gh is pronounced in the same way as dh, and hence g and d are liable to be mistaken—the one for the other. Ean had become s

RIDGES. Reefs of rocks   Ridge is sometimes a corruption of *ruigh*, slope

RIGGANHEAD. Fold on a gentle slope. *Chuid, cuid* aspirated, fold ; *ruighean*, diminutive of *ruigh*, slope.

RIGLEY HILL. Hill with a gently sloping side. *Ruigh*, lower slope of a hill ; *leth* (th silent), side

ROBIN'S WELL, for Robie's Well. *Roibeach*, overgrown with vegetation. *Roibeach* had become Robie

ROBINTIPSY'S PLANTATION   Wood on a rough bushy hill. Robintipsy's represents *Roibeach Thom Sithean*. Bushy hill. *Roibeach*, shaggy ; *thom, tom* aspirated, hill ; *sithean*, little hill. Th in *sithean* is silent and had been lost, and ean had been made y as a diminutive termination, normally, and s as a plural termination, abnormally. "Robie Thomson's Smiddy", the title of a song, is a corruption of this name with *suidhe*, place, added to it. *Suidhe* became Smiddy.

ROB'S WA'S. Rough place. *Roibean*, roughness, rough ; *bhaile, baile* aspirated, farm town, place. Ean was improperly made s.   Bh is equal to w, and by the loss of ile and the addition of euphonic s *bhaile* became wa's

ROCKVILLE, for *Baile Ruigh*. Town on a hillside. *Baile*, town ; *ruigh*, slope of a hill . *Baile* had been put last and made *bhaile*, pronounced vaile. Gh in *ruigh* had been made ch, which by loss of the aspirate became ruic, now made rock

ROGERS CLEUGH, for *Ruigh Airidh* Cleugh   Ravine of the slope on the shieling   *Ruigh*, slope ; *airidh*, shieling.

ROOK LAW. Slope of the hill. *Ruigh*, slope , *lamh*, hill.

ROTTEN CLEUGH. Ravine of the little round hill. *Rotan*, little round hill, cognate with rotundus (Latin), round

ROTTEN ROW BURN, for *Allt Rotan Rath*. Burn of the little round hill at a fold. *Allt*, burn , *rotan*, little round hill ; *rath*, (th silent), fold.

ROTTEN ROW   Row of houses at a round knoll. *Rotan*, round knoll.

ROUGH CLEUGH. Ravine on the slope of a hill. *Ruigh*, slope.

ROUNALL   Round figure.   Rondelle (French), round space. Or, *Chruinn Aill*, round hill. *Chruinn, cruinn* aspirated, round ; *aill*, hill.

ROWAN CLEUGH.   Ravine of the rowan-tree.   *Caorrunn,* rowan-tree.

RUCHLAW,   Slope of a hill.   *Ruigh,* slope; *lamh,* hill.

RUGGED KNOWES, RAGGED ROCK   Rugged and Ragged represent *Ruigh Chuid*   Slope of the fold   *Ruigh,* slope, *chuid, cuid* aspirated, fold.   C in ch, being silent, had been lost.

RULES LAW.   Rules is *Ruigh Lamhan.*   Slope of the little hill.   *Ruigh* (igh lost), slope; *lamhan* (amh lost), little hill. An in *lamhan* was erroneously made es instead of ie, and ru and les combined made rules   *Lamh,* hill, is a late addition explaining les in rules.   Mh, being silent, was lost, and la became law.

RUNSHAW RIG.   Wooded slope on a hill.   Run represents *ruighean* (gh silent), diminutive of *ruigh,* slope at the base of a hill.   Shaw means wood.   Rig is a contraction of *ruigh,* slope, which had been added to explain run after its meaning had been lost.

RYEHILL.   Slope of the hill.   *Ruigh,* slope.

SADDLE RIG.   Saddle and Rig in this name mean a round backed ridge between two burns, which is not the usual meaning *Ruigh,* slope of a hill where it extends into a plain.

SAINT AGNES.   Hill of the enclosure.   *Sithean,* little hill; *innis,* enclosure, fold.   Euphonic t was added to *sithean.*

SAINT CLEMENT'S WELL, for *Bhaile Sithean Clamhan.*   Town at a small hill frequented by kites.   *Bhaile, baile* aspirated, town; *sithean,* small hill; *clamhan,* kite.   Bh is equal to w, and *bhaile* became waile and afterwards wells by the addition of euphonic s.   *Sithean* lost ith, and by the addition of euphonic t it became saint.   *Clamhan* lost h, and by the addition of euphonic t it became clement.

SAINT MUNGO'S WELL.   Well on a hill with a fold on a shieling.   *Sitheàn,* little hill, *moine,* moor; *cuith,* fold.   *Sithean* lost th with its flanking vowels, and t was added for euphony, *moine* lost final e, and *cuith* lost th silent.   Cui became go, as in Glasgow, Linlithgow, Lesmahagow.

SALTCOATS, for *Seal Cuitan.*   Shiel at a small fold.   *Seal,* shiel, temporary residence; *cuitan,* diminutive of *cuit,* fold.   T in salt is a euphonic addition to l made because t frequently follows l. An of *cuitan* ought to have become ie and not s.

SALTON, for *Baile Samh.*   Pleasant town.   *Baile,* town; *Samh* (Irish), mild, beautiful.   Mh, being silent, had been lost, and l, an ancillary letter, had been inserted for euphony.

SAMUELSTON.   Town at a pleasant knoll.   *Samh* (Irish), pleasant; *mulan,* hillock.   An abnormally became s.

SANDERSDEAN, for *Dein Sithean Airidh.*   Dean of the hill on the shieling.   *Dein,* dean, den; *sithean,* small hill; *airidh,* shieling.   *Sithean* lost th and the flanking vowels.   S was inserted to form an English possessive.

SANDY HIRST.   Sandy thicket.   Hyrst (Anglo-Saxon), thicket, shrubby place

SANDY'S MILL. Mill at a little hill. *Sithean*, little hill.

SAUCHET WATER. Burn of the pleasant place. *Samhach*, pleasant , *aite*, place. With mh silent *samhach* is pronounced sauch. Final e is lost in names.

SAUGHY GRAIN. Quiet branch of a burn. *Samhach*, quiet ; grain (Scotch), branch of a burn.

SCARHILL. Hill rising to a rocky point. *Syor*, rock

SCORE HILL Pointed hill. *Sgor*, sharp-pointed rock

SCOUGHALL, for *Eas Gog Choill*. Burn of the fold on a hill *Eas*, burn , *gog*, fold ; *choill*, *coill* aspirated, hill Ea of *eas* had been lost

SCRAYMOOR. Sod moor *Sgrath*, turf, sod

SCULLINS CLEUGH, for *Sloc Eas Coillean* Gorge of the burn of the little hill. *Sloc*, gorge , *eas*, burn , *coillean*, little hill. *Eas* lost ea, and an of *coillean* was improperly changed to s

SEGGARSDEAN. Rough den where sedges grow *Garbh*, rough , *dein*, den , *seisg*, sedge, seg (Scotch)

SHEARNIE CLEUGH. Yawning ravine *Searnach* (Irish), yawning.

SHEIL RIG Slope on which there was a hut occupied in summer by persons in charge of cattle *Seal*, shiel, temporary residence ; *ruigh*, slope, supposed to mean ridge

SHERIFFHALL. Hill of the dark burn *Choill*, *coill* aspirated, hill ; *sear*, dark , *abh*, burn

SHERRIFFSIDE. Side of the black burn. *Sear*, dark , *abh*, water Side might represent *suidhe*, place.

SILVER HILL. Cattle hill. *Sealbhar*, cattle

SINK BRIDGE. Bridge at a little hill. *Sithean* (thea silent and lost), little hill Euphonic k was added to n

SKATERAW, for *Eas Cuit Rath* Burn at the fold. *Eas*, burn , *cuit*, fold , *rath*, fold, added to explain *cuit*.

SKEDSBUSH. Bush at the burn of the small fold *Eas*, burn , *cuidan*, small fold. An ought to have been made ie, not s.

SKELLIES, SGEILGAN. Plural of *sgeilg*, rock. G had become gh, equal to ie, and an normally became s.

SKID HALL, for *Eas Cuid* Hill Burn of the fold hill. *Eas*, burn , *cuid*, fold.

SKIMMER. Hill of ditches *Easgach*, full of ditches or marshes , *mur*, hill. Ach was lost.

SKINNER BURN Burn gushing out from a shieling. *Sginn*, to gush out ; *airidh*, shieling.

SLATEFORD. Ford with the river bed shod with trunks of trees laid longitudinally. *Slatach*, laid with rods.

SLAUGHTERCLEUGH, for *Eas Sliabh-Thir* Cleugh Ravine of the burn of the hill land. *Eas*, burn ; *sliabh-thir*, hill land (*sliabh*, hill ; *thir*, tir aspirated, land).

SLED HILL. Hill *Sliabh*, hill Or, hill near a main road. *Slighe*, road. Gh and dh have the same sound, and the one is liable to be mistaken for the other. *Slighe* might have become slidhe

SLEEPY KNOWE. Knoll on a hill. *Sliabh*, hill.

SLOEBIGGING Buildings on a height *Sliabh*, hill.

D

SMEATON. Small town. *Smiot*, small thing.

SMITHY PARK. Small park. *Smiotan*, small thing.

SMUDDLE HA. Hill giving off visible vapour. *Smuideil*, smoking ; *choill, coill* aspirated, hill. Smuddle Ha is on the east side of a hill. In a calm frosty morning in winter when the sun shines on it hoar frost is melted and evaporated, and when the vapour ascends into the cold air it is condensed and looks like smoke.

SMYLIE KNOWES. Small knolls. *Smeilach*, puny.

SNAILS CLEUGH, for *Sloc Eas Naimhdeil*. Gorge of the impetuous burn. *Sloc*, gorge ; *eas*, burn ; *naimhdeil*, vehemence, impetuosity.

SNEEP. Long slender point, resembling the neb of the snipe.

SNOWDON, for *Snadhach Dun*. Wet hill. *Snadhach*, watery ; *dun*, hill.

SOLAN CRAIG. Rock frequented by solan geese.

SOUN HOPE. Both words mean hill, but on the Ordnance Survey map they are placed over a ravine as if Hope meant a sheltered place. Soun is a corruption of *sithean* (th silent), hill ; and hope is *chop, cop* aspirated, hill.

SOUNDING BURN. Burn from a marshy place. *Sughanach*, watery. Euphonic d had been added to n.

SOUTHFIELD. Place of rich soil. *Suth*, juice, sap, fatness.

SOW. This name may have anciently been *Suidhe*, place. *Suidhe* is pronounced soo-ie. Many of the coast names indicate that the sea has encroached on the land.

SPA WELL. Well whose water is impregnated with carbonate of iron. Spa Wells are named after Spa in Belgium, where there are chalybeate wells.

SPARTLEDON EDGE. Flat-topped hill. *Spar*, an eminence flat on the top ; *tulach*, hill ; *dun*, hill ; *aod*, brae. In *aod* o is silent and d is pronounced as dg.

SPEEDY BURN. Burn of the waterhole where cattle drank. *Eas*, burn ; *puite*, well, drinking place.

SPILMERSFORD. Ford in the burn of the fold on the little hill. *Eas*, burn ; *peall*, fold, protected place ; *murean*, little hill. Ean had become s instead of ie.

SPITTAL. Shelter for travellers, or poor, aged, and infirm persons. Hospitalia (Latin), apartments for strangers.

SPITTALHALL. Hill where there was a hospital. *Choill, coill* aspirated, hill ; hospitalia (Latin), apartments for strangers.

SPITTALRIG. Slope of the spital. *Ruigh*, slope ; hospitalia (Latin), apartments for strangers, house for sick, aged, or infirm persons.

SPOTT. The name of a parish taken from a circular spot of ground, about a third of a mile in circumference, and three acres in extent. Anciently it had been a fold where cattle were penned and watched at night. On the Ordnance Survey maps it is called The Chesters, and it is said to have been a British fort.

SPRUCE CLEUGH, for *Eas Preas*. Ravine of the burn where bushes grow. *Eas*, burn ; *preas*, bush.

STABSTONE LOAN, for *Lian Baile Stabh*. Grassy place at a town near a fold   *Lian*, grassy plain ; *baile*, town , *stabh* (Irish), fold

STANESHILL WOOD   Wood of the hill where stones were quarried   Hall is *choill*, *coill* aspirated, hill.   C in ch is silent, and hoill became hall.

STANNYSCORE HILL, for *Sithean Syor* Hill   Hill with a rocky point   *Sithean*, corrupted into stany, little hill , *syor*, point of rock.   Ean had become y, normally

STEEL CLEUGH.   Ravine of a burn.   *Cleugh*, ravine , *steall*, burn, spring

STELLHOUSE   Protected fold.   *Stell*, protection , *chuith*, *cuith* aspirated, fold   C was lost, and th became sh, which lost h   Huis became house

STENTON, formerly Stanctown and Stanton.   Stone town.   In early times houses were nearly all built of clay or sods   To be built of stone was a distinction.

STEVENSON.   *Sithean Sithean*   Little hill   *Sithean*, little hill, which became steven by the change of th into bh, equal to v   To this had been added as an explanation another *sithean*, which became son by loss of th with its following vowel.

STING BANK, STING HILL.   Sting is *sithean*, small hill, with euphonic g added to it.

STOBSHIEL   Shiel at a pointed hill   *Stob*, pointed hill , *seal*, temporary summer residence, shiel.

STONELAWS.   Both parts of the name mean little hill.   *Sithean*, small hill , *lamhan*, small hill   *Sithean* became stean, which has been made stone.   An in *lamhan* is a diminutive termination, but it had been regarded as a plural and made s.

STONYPATH TOWER.   Tower on a hill growing birches.   *Sithean*, little hill , *beathach*, producing birches   *Sithhean* became stany, which is now stony.   *Beathach* became path as in Pathhead

STOT CLEUGH   Ravine from which vapour rises in a quiet frosty morning.   *Stoth*, steam

STRABAUCHLINY.   Big pool in alluvial ground   *Baghach* (gh silent), big , *linne*, pool , *srath*, alluvial ground

STRONG'S HOLE, for *Sron Choill*   Point of the hill   *Sron*, point, nose , *choill*, *coill* aspirated, hill   C had been lost

SUMMER HILL.   Wet hill.   *Sughmhor*, wet

SWARNIE CLEUGH   Little wet ravine   *Sugharan*, little wet place.   Gh is equal to y, and an became first na and then nie

SWINE ORCHARD   Wet Orchard   *Sughan* (gh silent), wet. The place is 40 feet above sea level

SYDSERF   Place on a black burn   *Suidhe*, place ; *sear* (Irish), dark, black , *abh*, water, burn

TABLE RINGS, for *Tamh Aill Ruighean*.   Dwelling on a hill with a slight slope.   *Tamh*, house ; *aill*, hill , *ruighean*, diminutive of *ruigh*, slope   Mh and bh are both equal to v.   Hence *tamh* had become *tebh*, which afterwards lost h   Ean of *ruighean* had improperly been made s, which had been appended to ing instead of being substituted for it

TANDERLANE. Grass-land at a small burn. *Lian*, grassy place; *tain*, water; *der* (Irish), small.

TANTALLON CASTLE. Castle on a hill at a small burn *Dun*, hill; t, euphonic addition to n, *allan*, small burn.

TAVERS CLEUGH. Ravine in which there was a shieling hut. *Tamh*, dwelling, residence, *airidh*, shieling.

TAY BURN. House at a burn. *Taigh*, house. Gh is equal to y

TENTERFIELD. Place at a river on a shieling. *Tain*, burn, river (Tyne); *airidh*, shieling.

THIEVES DIKE. Dike of the little fold. *Chuithan*, *cuithan* aspirated, little fold. Ch became th, and th became bh, which is equal to v. An was improperly made es instead of ie.

THISTLY CROSS. Crossing near a burn. *Uisge*, burn, water.

THORNTON. Hill town. *Charn*, carn aspirated, hill. Ch became th.

THORTER CLEUGH. Cross ravine. Thorter is a Scotch word meaning to cross. The name may, however, represent *Chort Airidh* Cleugh. Ravine of the fold on the shieling. *Chort*, cort aspirated, fold; *airidh*, shieling.

THREEP LAW, THREEPLAND. Hill. *Thriath*, *triath* aspirated, hill; *lamh*, hill; *lamhan*, small hill. In *lamhan* mh became silent and was lost, and euphonic d was added to n.

THURSTON, for *Thorran Dun*. Knoll on a hill. *Thorran*, *torran* aspirated, little hill; *dun*, hill An had been made s instead of ie.

THURSTON HIGH WOOD. Wood at a fold on Thurston. High is *chuith*, *cuith* aspirated, fold. C and th were lost, and hui is now high.

TINKER'S LEAP. Bend of the burn of the shieling. *Luib*, bend; *tain*, burn; *airidh*, shieling. Euphonic k had been added to n.

TIPPERSTONE RIG. Slope of the stone at a well *Ruigh*, slope; *tobar*, well. But stone might be for ton with s inserted to connect the two parts of the name.

TOD BURN. Warm burn. *Teothad* (th silent), warmth, heat.

TODDY KNOWES. High knolls. *Toghta*, raised up.

TODLAW RIG. Ridge of the hill of the fox. *Ruigh*, slope, erroneously thought to mean ridge; tod (Scotch), fox; *lamh*, hill.

TOM'S LINN. Waterfall on the hill *Tom*, hill; *linne*, fall, pool S made *tom* possessive.

TORNESS. Point ending in a steep round hill. *Ness*, point; *torr*, steep round flat-topped hill.

TOWNHEAD. Hill head. *Dun*, hill.

TRABRONN. Side of a stream. *Traigh*, side, *braon*, burn.

TRAPRAIN LAW. Hill of the fold. *Triath*, hill; *rathan*, fold; *lamh*, hill. Th in *triath* became ph, and h was lost, th in *rathan* is silent; *lamh* was added to explain *triath*.

TRINDLE BONNY. Small place at the bottom of a small hill. *Triathan* (th silent), small hill; *lamh*, (mh silent), hill, *bonnan*,

TRIPSLAW. Both parts mean hill. *Triathan*, diminutive of *triath*, hill, *lamh*, hill Th became ph, and h was lost. An was improperly made s instead of ie

TUN LAW. Hill *Dun*, hill; *lamh*, hill. After *dun* had been corrupted law had been added to explain it.

TYNE. River. *Tain*, water.

TYNNINGHAME. Dwelling near a small stream (Tyne) *Tainan*, diminutive of *tain*, water; ham (Frisian), home

UGSTON RIG. Town on a brae. *Uchd*, brae; *ruigh*, slope. S represents a sound like g or ɟ following d. *Ruigh* explains *uchd*

VEITCH PLACE. Place where birches grew. *Bheith, beith* aspirated, birch. Bh is equal to v, and th had been strengthened by inserting c. Veitch is also a personal name.

VINEYARD. Rough hill. *Garbh*, rough, *bheinn, beinn* aspirated, hill

WALDEAN. Town near a den. *Bhaile, baile* aspirated, town, *dein*, den, dean. Bh being equal to w, and final e being dropped, *bhaile* became wal.

WALLACE'S CAVE, WALLACE'S CLEUGH Wallace's is for *Easan Bhuaile* Little burn of the fold. *Easan*, little burn, with an changed to s instead of ie; *bhuaile, buaile* aspirated, fold Cave, if Gaelic, is *cabh* (bh equal to v), hollow; and cleugh is a ravine eroded by a burn.

WALLY CLEUGH, WALLYFORD. The exact meaning of these names is uncertain. Wally might represent either *bhaile, baile* aspirated, town; or *bhuaile, buaile* aspirated, fold. Cleugh is a ravine excavated by a burn. Bh is equal to w, and both *bhaile* and *bhuaile* might become wally.

WAMPHRAY, for *Chuit Abh Rath*. Fold at a burn *Chuit, cuit* aspirated, fold, *abh*, burn, *rath*, fold *Chuit* became white, which was turned into Gaelic by *bhan, ban* aspirated, white. Bh is equal to w and *bhan* became first wan and next wam, *abh* became ph, and *rath* became ray. *Rath* had been added to give the meaning of the first part after *chuit* was corrupted.

WANTONWA'S, for *Bhaile Chuitail*. Town at a fold. *Bhaile, baile* aspirated, town; *chuitail, cuitail* aspirated, fold *Chuitail* became whitehill Whitehill was afterwards turned into Gaelic by *bhandun*, white hill (*bhan, ban* aspirated, white; *dun*, hill). Bh is equal to w and *bhandun* became wanton *Bhaile* became wale, afterwards made wall, which is now wa's, s being added for euphony.

WATCH LAW. Watch hill. *Lamh*, hill

WATTIE'S HOWE Main road howe *Chatha, catha* aspirated, drove road, main road. Ch had become bh, equal to w S made Wattie possessive

WAUGHTON. Hillock *Uchdan*, brow of a hill, hillock.

WEAK LAW Hill of the circle *Bheachd, beachd* aspirated, ring, circle, fold; *lamh*, hill Bh is equal to w

WEATHER LAW, WEATHERLY, for *Lamh Chuith Airidh*. Hill of the fold on a shieling *Lamh*, hill, *chuith, cuith* aspirated, fold; *airidh*, shieling Mh became w in the first name and y in the second ; ch became bh, equal to w ; and idh, being silent, was lost.

WEIRD'S WOOD.　Wood with the tops of the trees looking as if the points had been shorn off.　*Bhearrta, bearrta* aspirated, shorn.

WELL HAG WOOD.　Well at the jackdaws' wood.　*Chathag, cathag* aspirated, jackdaw.　In *chathag* c and tha being silent had been lost, leaving hag.　*Cathag* (th silent), resembles the cry of the jackdaw.

WELL HILL.　Hill of the fold.　*Choill, coill* aspirated, hill ; *bhuaile, buaile* aspirated, fold.　Bh is equal to w, and *bhuaile* had become well.

WEST HOPES.　West little hill.　*Chopan, copan* aspirated, little hill.　C silent was lost, and an was improperly made es instead of ie.

WEST STEEL.　West burn.　*Steall*, gushing spring, stream.

WHALE ROCK.　Rock of the fold.　*Fal*, fold.　Fisher people call a whale a fal, and hence has arisen confusion as to the meaning of the words whale and fal in names of places.

WHARE BURN.　Burn terminating at a spit of land.　*Bhear, bear* aspirated, point.　Bh may become u, v, w, or y.

WHEATRIG, for *Ruigh Chuit*.　Slope of the fold.　*Ruigh*, slope ; *chuit, cuit* aspirated, fold.　Ch became wh.

WHIM.　Hill.　*Thom, tom* aspirated, hill.　Th had become wh, and o had become i.　Gullane Hill is the Whim.

WHIPPING TREE.　*Cheapan Triath*.　Little place on a hill. *Cheapan, ceapan* aspirated, small place ; *triath*, hill.　Ch became wh, and ath was lost.

WHITBERRY POINT.　Small point of land at a fold.　*Bioran*, small point ; *chuit, cuit* aspirated, fold.　An became y, normally, and *chuit* became white, now whit.

WHITE CASTLE, WHITE CLEUGH, WHITE KNOWE, WHITE SANDS.　In all these names the first word represents *Chuit, cuit* aspirated, fold, which by corruption became white.　White Castle is supposed to have been a British fort, but the first part shows that it was a fold.　White Cleugh means ravine of the fold, White Knowe is knoll of the fold, White Sands means fold on a sandy shore.

WHITE SLED.　Fold.　Originally *Chuitail, cuitail* aspirated, fold.　*Chuitail* became whitehill, and hill was afterwards made *sliabh*, hill.　Bh was changed to dh and h was lost.

WHITEADDER.　Fold on a shieling.　*Chuitail, cuitail* aspirated, fold ; *airidh*, shieling.　*Chuitail* was corrupted into whitehill, and hill was subsequently turned into Gaelic by *aod*, hill, brae. *Aod* and air of *airidh* made adder.

WHITEHILL.　Fold.　Originally *Chuitail, cuitail* aspirated, fold.　*Chuitail* was corrupted into whitehill.

WHITEKIRK, WHITELAW.　Both names were originally *chuitail, cuitail* aspirated, fold.　*Chuitail* became whitehill.　Hill was afterwards made *creag* in one name, and *lamh* in the other.　*Creag* became kirk and *lamh* became law.

WHITELOCH.　Loch at a fold.　*Loch*, lake ; *chuit, cuit* aspirated, fold. *Chuit* was corrupted into white, which was supposed to be an English adjective and put before *loch*

WHITTINGHAM, WHITTINGHAME. Dwelling-place at a small fold *Chuitan, cuitan* aspirated, small fold , ham (Frisian), home Ch became wh, and an became ing.

WIDE HOPE, for *Chop Chuid* Hill of the fold *Chop, cop* aspirated, hill ; *chuid, cuid* aspirated, fold. *Chop* became hope, and *chuid* became wide The Ordnance Survey map has the name on a river valley as if it meant a wide shelter.

WIDOW'S KNOWE Knoll of the little fold *Chuidan, cuidan* aspirated, little fold Ch became bh, equal to w ; an became ow instead ie ; and s was added because an is sometimes a plural termination

WIGHTMAN HILL. Hill of the fold. *Chuitail, cuitail* aspirated, fold *Chuitail* became whitehill and hill was afterwards turned into Gaelic by *man*, hill White also underwent a change and was made wight, meaning man, to make it identical with *man* the last part, though it meant hill One man was Gaelic and the other English.

WILKIE HAUGH Haugh in a corner. *Uileann*, corner. Wilkie is a diminutive of William, with which *uileann* had been confounded.

WILLIAMSTON. Place in a crook of a burn *Uileann*, nook.

WINDING LAW, for *Lamh Bheinnan* Hill. *Lamh*, hill ; *bheinnan, beinnan* aspirated, little hill. *Lamh* is an explanation of *bheinnan*

WINDY LAW Little hill. *Bheinnan, beinnan* aspirated, little hill Bh is equal to w, an normally became y, and d was added to n for euphony, all which produced windy. *Lamh*, law, was added to windy to explain it after its meaning had been lost.

WINDY MAINS, for *Bheinnan Manan*, both of which mean little hill *Bheinnan, beinnan* aspirated, little hill ; *manan*, diminutive of *man*, hill. Bh is equal to w, euphonic d had been inserted, and final an had normally became y. An of *manan* had abnormally become s, instead of ie.

WINDY SLACK. Windy gorge between two hills *Sloc*, gorge

WINDYGHOUL Windy ridge *Gobhal*, ridge. G had been aspirated and had then been pronounced like the y which preceded it. Bh is equal to ou.

WINE CELLAR, for *Bheinn Seal Airidh* Hill of the hut on a shieling *Bheinn, beinn* aspirated, hill , *seal*, shiel, hut ; *airidh*, shieling, summer pasture.

WINTERFIELD, for *Achadh Chuithan Airidh*. Field at a little fold on a shieling. *Achadh*, field , *chuithan, cuithan* aspirated, little fold , *airidh*, shieling. *Chuithan* lost ch and tha, and euphonic t was added to n. *Airidh* lost idh.

WINTON. Town on a hill. *Bheinn, beinn* aspirated, hill. Bh is equal to w, and *bheinn* had been pronounced . in

WITCHES KNOWE, WITCHES SYKE Knoll of the little fold and Syke at the little fold Witches was originally *kuthan cuithan* aspirated, little fold Ch was changed to bh, equal to w; th was strengthened by inserting c; and an was wrongly made es

WOLF CLEUGH, WOLFSTAR. Cave of the ravine, and Cave of the cliff. *Uamh*, cave. Mh is equal to v, which much resembles f in sound. Cleugh is a burn ravine, and star is *stor*, cliff.

WOODHALL. Hill of the wood. *Choill, coill* aspirated, hill. In modern Gaelic *coill* means wood, so the first part may be a translation of the second.

WOOL HILL. Hill on which there is a turn in a parish boundary. *Uileann*, angle, corner. Eann had became ie and had been lost.

WOOLYLANDS. Little hill between two burns *Uileann*, angle, corner, *lamhan*, little hill. Uile became wool, and ann became y; *lamhan* lost mh, d was added to n for euphony, and s was also added because an was supposed to be a plural termination.

WRECKED CRAIGS Grey rocks. *Riabhach*, grey.

WRITERSPATH BURN. Burn on the slope of a shieling, on which birches grow. *Ruigh*, slope; *airidh*, shieling; *beath*, birch

YARROW. Shieling. *Airidh*, shieling.

YEARN GILL. Gap of the burn valley. *Bhearn, bearn* aspirated, gap; *gill*, burn valley. Bh is usually equal to v or w. Here it has become y. *Gill* is supposed to be a Norse word, but it is more likely a local Gaelic word.

YELLOW CRAIG. Fold *Chuitail, cuitail* aspirated, fold. *Chuitail* became whitehill, which was turned into Gaelic by *ghealach creay*, white hill (*ghealach, gealach* aspirated, white; *creag*, hill, craig). Gh is equal to y and *ghealach* became yallaw in Scotch, made yellow in English.

YELLOW CRAIGS. Fold *Chuitail, cuitail* aspirated, fold. *Chuitail* became whitehill, which was turned into Gaelic by *ghealach creagan*, white hill (*ghealach, gealach* aspirated, white; *creagan*, diminutive of *creag*, craig, hill). By mistake an was made s as if it had been a plural termination. Gh is equal to y and *ghealach* became yallaw in Scotch, which was made yellow in English.

YELLOW MAN. Fold *Chuitail, cuitail* aspirated, fold. *Chuitail* became whitehill, which was turned into Gaelic by *ghealach man*, white hill (*ghealach, gealach* aspirated, white, *man*, hill). Gh is equivalent to y, and *ghealach* became yallaw in Scotch, made yellow in English.

YESTER. Burn of the strath. *Eas*, burn, *srath*, alluvial river valley

YETTS. Birches. *Bheathan, beathan* aspirated, birch trees. Bh became y, and an normally became s This produced yeaths, now made yetts As a personal name the spelling is yeats.

YOUNGS' KNOWE. Knoll of the little hill. *Dhunan, dunan* aspirated, little hill. Dh is equal to y, an was improperly made s, and g was added to n for euphony.

ZADLEE. Grassy place on a brae above a burn. Ley (Scotch), grass-land, *eas*, burn; *aod*, brae. *Eas* is represented by the letter z

PLACE NAMES
OF
WEST LOTHIAN

GAELIC
PLACE NAMES
OF
WEST LOTHIAN

BY

JOHN MILNE, LL.D.

PUBLISHED FOR THE AUTHOR BY
McDOUGALL'S EDUCATIONAL COMPANY, LIMITED.
LONDON: 8 FARRINGDON AVENUE, E.C.
EDINBURGH: 1 AND 2 ST. JAMES SQUARE.

PLACE NAMES OF
WEST LOTHIAN.

ABERCORN. Infall of the Cornie burn. *Aber*, infall; see Cornie Burn.

ADAMBRAE. Ford Ford at a brae. *Aodann*, brae The second part is a translation of the first

ALMOND. Burn of the hill. *All*, burn; *monadh*, hill.

ALMONDELL. Valley of the Almond. Dell (English), dale.

ARMADALE Temporary residence on a field near a river. *Airidh*, shiel, hut on summer pasture; *na*, of the, *dail*, riverside field

AUCHINHARD. Place on a hill *Achadh*, place; *an*, of the; *ard*, hill.

AULDCATHIE. Burn near a main road. *Allt*, burn, *catha*, drove road, through road.

AVON BRIDGE Bridge over the Avon. *Abhainn*, water, stream. *Abhainn* is also spelt *amhainn*, which shows connection with amnis (Latin), river

BACK OF MOSS. Both parts have the same meaning, *Bac*, peat-moss.

BAILIES MUIR. Town on a muir, *Baile*, town.

BALBARDIE Town in a meadow *Baile*, town; *bardan*, small meadow.

BALDERSTON, for *Baile Airidh*. Town on a shieling. *Baile*, town, *airidh*, shieling. D is a euphonic addition to l, s forms a possessive, and ton is a translation of *baile*.

BALGORNIE Town of fire brands *Baile*, town; *gornan*, plural of *gorn*, fire brand. Signals might have been made at this place by waving torches at night.

BALGREEN Town of the sun, or sunny town *Baile*, town, *greine*, genitive of *grian*, sun

BALLENCRIEFF. Town of the fold. *Baile*, town; *an*, of the, *crubh*, fold Bh had become ph, equal to f.

BALMUIR Town on a muir *Baile*, town

BALVORMIE. Town where there was a big balance. *Baile*, town; *mhor*, feminine of *mor*, big, *meidh*, balance. Mh is equal to v, and dh is equal to ie.

BANGOUR KNOWES, for *Cnocan Cuit Gobhar*. Knoll of the fold of goats *Cnocan*, diminutive of *cnoc*, hill, *cuit*, fold, *gobhar*, goat. S of knowes represents an of cnocan, erroneously thought to be a plural termination. *Cuit* became white, which was turned into Gaelic by *ban*, white. Bh in *gobhar* sounds ou.

B

BANK BURN. Burn at a fold. *Chuit*, fold, corrupted into white, which had afterwards been turned into Gaelic by *ban*, white. K is a euphonic addition to an.

BANKHEAD. The name had originally been *Chuit*, *cuit* aspirated, fold, which had been corrupted into white, and this had been turned into Gaelic by *ban*, white, with k added for euphony. To explain bank *chuid*, *cuid* aspirated, fold, had been added to it, but c silent had been lost and then huid had become head.

BANKHEAD. This is sometimes an English name, meaning a farm town at a level place at the head of a bank.

BANKS. Fold. *Chuit*, *cuit* aspirated, fold, corrupted into white, which was made in Gaelic *ban*, white. Some persons, however, made it *can*, white, and the two were combined into *bancan*. An was improperly regarded as a plural termination and was changed to s, which produced bancs, now banks, but the name is not appropriate for the place.

BARBAUCHLAW, for *Barr Baghach Lamh*. Point of the big hill. *Barr*, point; *baghach*, big; *lamh*, hill.

BARESHEIL. Knowe. *Baresheil*, for *Bair Seal*. Road to a shiel. *Bair*, road; *Seal*, shiel, hut on a shieling.

BARNBOUGLE. Barn at a cow-byre. *Buaigheal*, cow-stall.

BARNS. Gap. *Bearnas*, gap, long hollow.

BARON'S HILL. Hill with a gap. *Bearnas*, gap.

BARRACKS. Place at a greater elevation than its neighbours. *Barrachas*, pre-eminence.

BARREN CRAIG. Hill with a gap. *Creag*, hill; *bearna*, gap, hollow in the skyline.

BATHGATE. Windy cow-house. *Bathaich*, cow-byre; *gaothach*, windy.

BEAD PIT. Place of birch-trees. *Beath*, birch; *pit*, place.

BEATLIE, for *Beatlach*. Place of birch-trees.

BEDFORMIE. Green grove. *Bad*, wood, grove; *gorma*, green, blue. *Gorma* had become *corma*, by aspiration *chorma*, which would readily become forma. In Aberdeenshire ch in names is frequently pronounced as f.

BEECRAIGS. Little hill growing birches. *Creagan*, little hill; *beith*, birch. An had become s instead of ie. Th in *beith* is silent.

BELLS BRIDGE, BELL'S KNOWE, BELLS MILL, BELLSTONE. In these names the first part is *buaile*, cattlefold. S had been inserted to make it possessive and connect it with the second part.

BELSYD. Site of a cowfold. *Suidhe*, place; *buaile*, milking fold.

BENHAR. Hill of the shieling. *Beinn*, hill; *airidh*, shieling. Euphonic h had been prefixed to *airidh*, and idh had been lost.

BENTHEAD. Hill of the fold. *Beinn*, hill; *cuidh*, *cuid* aspirated, fold. Euphonic t had been added to n, and c in ch had been lost, being silent.

BENTS   Little hill.   *Beinntan,* diminutive of *beinn,* hill. An had improperly been made s.

BEUGH BURN.   Noisy burn.   *Beuchd,* noise, roar.

BICKERTON BURN.   Burn of the town where wooden bowls and cups were made.   *Biceir,* cap, bowl, cup.   These were made of alder-wood and could be made only where the alder-tree grew.

BINKS.   Fold   *Chuitail, cuitail* aspirated, fold, corrupted into whitehill, which was afterwards turned into Gaelic by *beinncan,* whitehill (*beinn,* hill, *can,* white)   An of *can* was regarded as a plural termination and changed to s.   This added to beinnc made beinncs, now become binks.

BINNS.   Little hill.   *Beinnan,* diminutive of *beinn,* hill.   An was wrongly made s instead of ie.

BINNY CRAIG   Little hill.   *Beinnan,* little hill, *creag,* hill   An became y   *Creag* had been added as an explanation of *beinnan.*

BIRDS MILL   Mill in a meadow.   *Bard,* meadow.

BIRNYHILL   Hill with a gap   *Bearna,* gap

BISHOP BRAE.   Brae of the birchy hill.   *Beithach,* abounding in birches, *chop, cop* aspirated, hill   Th had become sh; ach had been lost, and c of *chop* had been lost

BLACKCRAIG.   Hill on which there was a milking fold.   *Creag,* hill; *bleoghann,* milking   Ann had become ie and it had been lost.

BLACKFAULDS.   Small enclosed fields whose walls were constructed of black mossy sods   Black is sometimes a corruption of *bleoghann,* milking, or *bliochd,* milk.

BLACKLAWS.   Little black hill   *Lamhan,* diminutive of *lamh,* hill.   Mh is equal to u, but an should not have been made s.

BLACKNESS.   Black point   *Ness,* point   The rocks at the point are igneous and dark   In Gaelic speaking times *ness* had been pronounced nesh.

BLACKRIDGE.   Milking place on the slope of a hill   *Bleoghann,* milking, *ruigh,* slope

BLACKSHILLS, for *Coillean Bleoghann*   Knoll where cows were milked   *Coillean,* diminutive of *coill,* hill; *bleoghann,* milking. Neither ean nor ann is a plural termination and they should not have been made s.

BLAWHORN   Warm hill.   *Blath,* warm; *charn, carn* aspirated, hill.   C silent has been lost.

BLAWLOAN.   Warm grassy place in front of a house.   *Blath,* warm, *lon,* meadow, grassy place   In England loan is a grassy lane, in Scotland it is an uncultivated grassy place in front of a house.

BLUE BRAE   Hill of milk.   *Braigh,* hill; *bliochd,* milk. When applied to small near hills blue means place where cows were milked.

BOAR STONE   Big stone.   *Borr,* big.

BOGHALL   Farm town at a bog.   The kitchen was the hall of a farm house.

BOGYATES. Bog of the little fold. *Bog*, wet marshy place ; *chuitan, cuitan* aspirated, little fold. Ch had become gh, equal to y, and an had by mistake been made es instead of ie.

BONHARD. Bottom of the hill. *Bonn*, base ; *ard*, hill.

BONNYTOWNSIDE. Place in a hollow at the foot of a hill. *Bonnan*, diminutive of *bonn*, bottom ; *suidhe*, place. An normally became y.

BONSIDE. Place at the bottom of a hill. *Bonn*, bottom ; *suidhe*, place, site.

BORROWSTON. Town on a small hill. *Bruchan*, small hill. An had improperly become s, and this combining with ch had made bruchs, now become borrows.

BORROWSTOUN MAINS. Farm occupied by the proprietor of Borrowstoun. Terrae Dominicales (Latin), proprietor's lands. Terrae, lands ; dominicales, belonging to a landlord. In passing through French into English dominicales became domains, which in Scotch is now mains.

BORROWSTOUNNESS, for *Ness Bhaile Bruchan*. Point of the town on a small hill. *Ness* (pronounced nesh in Gaelic), point ; *baile*, town ; *bruchan*, small hill. *An* was improperly made s, and bruchs became borrows. Borrowstounness is often contracted to Bo'ness.

BOSLEM WELL. Well at a low hill. *Bos*, low ; *lamh*, hill.

BOWDEN, for *Bo Dun*. Cow hill. *Bo*, cow ; *dun*, hill. The "Fort" shown on the hill in maps had anciently been a great cowfold.

BOWGATE. Arched gate.

BRAES. Steep slopes. *Braigh*, hill.

BRAND'S QUARRY. Quarry at a burn. *Braon*, burn. D had been added for euphony, and also s because aon was wrongly regarded as a plural termination.

BREICH. Hill. *Bruch*, hill.

BROADLAW. Both parts mean hill. *Braid*, hill ; *lamh*, hill.

BROADYATES. Hill of the little fold. *Braid*, hill ; *chuitan, cuitan* aspirated, little fold. Ch became gh equal to y, and an was improperly made es instead of ie.

BROW. Hill. *Bruch*, hill.

BROWNHILL. Hill of the mountain burn. *Braon*, hill burn.

BROXBURN. Burn from the small hill. *Bruchan*, small hill. An was improperly made s instead of ie. Bruchs became first brux and then brox.

BRUCEFIELD. Hill field. *Bruch*, hill.

BRUNTON. Town at a burn. *Braon*, hill burn.

BUCHANS. Rocks which cause a loud roaring noise in the sea in a storm. *Beucach*, noisy, roaring.

BUGHTKNOWES. Hut for sheep on a knoll. *Buth*, hut, bught ; *cnocan*, knoll. An had wrongly been regarded as a plural termination.

BULLION WELL. Well at a small fold. *Buailean*, diminutive of *buaile*, fold.

BURGHMUIR. Muir belonging to the burgh of Linlithgow, to which all the burgesses had the right to send cattle.

BURN CRAIGS. Rocks at a burn. *Creagan,* plural of *creag,* rock. *Creagan* might be the diminutive of *creag,* hill.

BURNFOOT. Burn mouth.

BURNHEAD. Burn of the fold. *Braon,* hill burn, *chuid, cuid* aspirated, fold. C in ch was lost.

BURNHOUSE. Burn of the fold *Braon,* burn, *chuith, cuith* aspirated, fold. Ch became sh, and h was lost, producing huis, now house.

BURNSHOT. Small farm at a burn *Sgot,* shot, farm Sometimes the diminutive termination eag is corrupted into shot as in *claiseag,* small deep hollow, which has become clayshot.

BURNWIND Burn of the hill. *Braon,* burn, *bheinn, beinn* aspirated, hill. Bh is equal to w.

BUSHYLAW. Bushy hill. *Lamh,* hill

BUTLAW. House on a hill. *Buth,* house, *lamh,* hill.

BUTTER WELL Well at a house on a shieling *Buth,* house; *airidh* (idh silent), shieling.

BYCOTE, for *Cuit Ba'iche.* Fold at a cow-byre. *Cuit,* fold; *ba'iche,* cow-house, byre

BYRES Cow-houses. In Gaelic *Bathaichean,* plural of *bathaich,* cow-byre.

CAMPHILL. Crooked burn *Cam,* crooked, *pholl, poll* aspirated, pool, burn. *Poll* is aspirated because it follows its adjective.

CANNIEWELL SLACK. Slack at the head of the town *Ceann,* head; *a',* of the; *bhaile, baile* aspirated, town; *sloc,* gorge, narrow valley. The slack is between two hills where there is not a well.

CANTIES. Small hill. *Ceanntan,* diminutive of *ceann,* head, with euphonic t inserted. An normally became ie, but it was also made s by some, and both ie and s were added to ceannt.

CAPIES POINT. Small head. *Ceapan,* diminutive of *ceap,* head. An had by some been regarded as a diminutive and by others as a plural termination, and both ie and s had been added to ceap.

CAIRNEYHEAD. Little hill of the fold. *Carnan,* little hill; *chuid, cuid* aspirated, fold C in ch was lost.

CAIRNIE. *Carnan,* little hill. An normally became ie

CAIRN-NAPLE, for *Carn a' Peall.* Hill of the protected fold. *Carn,* hill; *a',* of the, *peall,* peel, protected place. Sometimes when a fold was made by a ring of tree-trunks, mats and hides were attached to the outside for a protection against wind and rain

CAPPERS, for *Ceap Airidhean* Hill of the small shieling. *Ceap,* head, hill, *airidhean,* diminutive of *airidh,* shieling Ean had improperly been regarded as a plural termination

CAPUTHALL. Hill of the road passing the fold. *Choill, coill* aspirated, fold; *cath,* drove road: *chuit, cuit* aspirated, fold Ch of *chuit* had become ph, but h had been lost.

CARL CAIRNIE. Witch hillock. Carl (English), wizard, witch ; *carnan*, little hill. An became ie.

CARLEDUBS, for *Cathair Lamh Dubhan*. Hill of darkness. *Cathair*, hill ; *lamh*, hill ; *dubhan*, darkness. An became s.

CARLOWRIE, for *Cathair Lughmhor Abhainn*. Hill of the rapid burn. *Cathair*, hill ; *lughmhor*, swift ; *abhainn*, burn. All the aspirated letters and some of the vowels had been lost. Ainn had become ie, which had afterwards been lost.

CARMEL HILL. Carmel is for *Garbh Meall*, rough hill. *Garbh*, rough, *meall*, hill.

CARRIBBER, for *Carr Ruigh Airidh*. Projecting part of the slope of a shieling hill. *Carr*, projection from a hill ; *ruigh*, slope ; *airidh* shieling. Gh had become bh, and h had been lost. Idh, being silent, had been lost.

CARRIDEN. Rocky den. *Carrach*, rocky ; *dein*, den.

CARSE OF KINNEIL, KINNEIL KERSE. Alluvial low grounds at Kinneil. *Catharan*, plural of *cathar*, wet flat ground. Th with its antecedent vowel had been lost, and an became s. The Carse of Kinneil was under the sea till the formation of the 25-feet beach by the elevation of the land.

CARSIE HILL. Projecting rocks on a hill. *Carr*, shelf of rock ; *sith* (th silent), hill.

CASTLE CRAIG. Castle hill. *Creag*, hill.

CASTLETHORN. Castle hill. Thorn is *Charn*, *carn* aspirated, hill. Ch had become th.

CATHLAW. Hill over which a road passed. *Cath*, road, drove road ; *lamh*, hill.

CAULD BURN. Rapid burn. *Callaidh*, active, nimble.

CAULDCOATS, CAULDHAME, CAULD WELLS. In these names cauld represents *cuil*, nook. Coats is *cuitan*, little fold, with an made s instead of ie. Hame is *thom* (t silent), *tom* aspirated, hill. Wells is *bhailean*, *bailean* aspirated, little town. Bh became w, and ean became s instead of ie.

CAULDIMMERY. Back of the little ridge. *Cul*, back, with euphonic d ; *imirean*, little ridge. Ean became y.

CAUSTON, for *Baile Cobhan*. Town in a hollow. *Baile*, town ; *cobhan*, hollow. Bh is equal to ou, and an had improperly been changed to s instead of ie.

CAW BURN. Burn of the hollow. *Cabh*, hollow. Bh is equal to ou.

CHAMPANY. Old fold. *Sean*, old ; *chuit*, *cuit* aspirated, fold, afterwards corrupted into white. This was turned into Gaelic by *baine*, whiteness, white. Se is pronounced she, nb often becomes mb, and *seanbaine* would readily have become shambaine, to be afterwards made champany.   [flowery.

CHAMPFLEURIE. Flowery field. Champ (Fr.), field ; fleuri (F.),

CHANCE PIT. Pit at a sheep fold. *Fhangan*, *fangan* aspirated, small fank. Fh became ch, g was lost, and an regarded as a plural termination was made s (now ce), which was added to chan. *Fhangan* has sometimes become change, as in Change-hill, Changehouse.

CHARLES'S BRIDGE. Bridge at a black fold. *Sear,* dark; *lios,* fold. *Sear* is pronounced shar.

CHESTER LAW. Hill where there was anciently a fortified cattlefold, supposed to have been a Roman fort. Castra (Latin), camp, *lamh,* hill.

CHUCKETHALL. Black fold hill. *Dubh,* black; *cuit,* fold; *choill, coill* aspirated, hill.

CITY, for *Suidhe*   Place.

CLAPPERTONHALL. Farm house in a muddy place *Clabar,* puddle, mire. The place is near a ford, and Clapperton may represent *clacharan,* stepping stones, with ch changed to ph and h dropped.

CLARENDON. Open broad space before a hill. *Clar,* clear broad space; *an,* of the; *dun,* hill.

CLOVE QUARRY. Quarry in a rough place. *Clumach,* rough.

CLOVEN CRAIG. Hill frequented by kites in search of mice, beetles, etc. *Clamhan,* kite, *creag,* hill. Mh is equal to v.

COCK HILL. The second part is a translation of the first. *Cnoc,* hill.

COCKLE BURN, for Cock Hill Burn. Burn of the hill. *Cnoc,* hill. *Cnoc* had lost n.

COCKLERUE. Slope of a hill   *Ruigh,* slope; *cnoc,* hill. Le represents hill, the translation of *cnoc.*

COCKMUIR. Muir on a hill. *Cnoc,* hill.

COLINSHIEL   Hut on a small hill. *Coillean,* diminutive of *coill,* hill; *seal* (pronounced shal), temporary residence on summer pasture. In Gaelic *sealan,* shieling, means summer pasture away from cultivated land; and *seal,* shiel, means a hut in which those in charge of cattle lived.

COLT HILL   Little hill   *Coilltean,* diminutive of *coill,* hill. Ean had become ie and had been lost.

CORBIEHALL. Hill of the fold. Corbie was originally *chuitail,* fold, corrupted into whitehill, which was turned into Gaelic by *corban,* white hill (*cor,* hill; *ban,* white)   Subsequently an was regarded as a diminutive termination and changed to ie. Hall represents *choill, coill* aspirated, hill, in which c had been lost.

CORNIE BURN. Burn from a little hill   *Carnan,* diminutive of *carn,* hill. An normally became ie.

COTMUIR   Muir of the fold   *Cuit,* fold.

COUCH. Fold. *Cuith,* fold. Th had become ch.

COUSLAND. Hill of the fold. *Lamhan,* hill; *cuithan,* diminutive of *cuith,* fold. Th is silent, and an had been made s instead of ie. Mh in *lamhan* is silent, and euphonic d had been added to an

COUSTON. Town in a hollow. *Cobhan,* hollow. Bh is equal to ou, and an had improperly been made s.

COW CRAGS, COW HILL, COWHILL. Originally *Cuithail,* fold. Th is silent, and cui had become cow. Ail had been thought to be *aill,* hill, and had been made *creagan,* little hill in the first and hill in the other two. *Creagan* had afterwards been made craigs, an being erroneously regarded as a plural termination. Ancient folds are now supposed to have been Roman forts.

COWDENHEAD. Cowden is *cuidan*, little fold; and head is *chuid, cuid* aspirated, fold, which had been added to cowden to tell its meaning.

CRAIG BRAE, CRAIGEND, CRAIGHEAD, CRAIGMAILING, CRAIG-MARRY, CRAIGMILL, CRAIGTON. The first part of the names is *creag*, hill. Head is *chuid, cuid* aspirated, fold, with c dropped; mailing is *meallan*, little hill; marry is *murean*, little hill, with ean made y; mill is the second form of *meall*, hill.

CRAIGENGALL. Little hill on which there was a stone pillar. *Creagan*, small hill; *gall*, monumental stone pillar.

CRAIGIE, CRAIGIEHALL. Craigie is *creagan*, small hill, with an made ie. Hall is *choill, coill* aspirated, hill, with c silent in ch dropped.

CRAIGS. Hillock. *Creagan*, diminutive of *creag*, hill, rock. It might also be the plural of *creag* and mean hills or rocks.

CRAMOND. Hill of the fold made with wattles. *Cra*, wattled fold.

CRANE HILL. Hill of the tree. *Crann*, tree.

CRAWHILL. Hill of the fold. *Cra*, fold made with wattles.

CRAWSTANE. Stone at a fold made with wattles. Stane might be ton, town, with s added to craw to connect the two parts.

CRINKLE BURN. Burn of the round hill. *Cruinn*, round; *choill, coill* aspirated, hill.

CROFTFOOT, CROFTHEAD. Both names mean knoll at a fold. *Croit*, croft, knoll, spot of grass. Foot is for *chuit, cuit* aspirated, fold, with ch made ph, which is f. Head is *chuid, cuid* aspirated, fold, with c of ch dropped because silent.

CROFTMALLOCH. Small piece of land on which there are humps. *Croit*, croft; *meallach*, abounding in little hills.

CROMYTY FAULDS. Small enclosed fields on the side of a hill. *Cromadh* (Irish), side of a hill.

CROSSALL. Cross on the hill. *Crois*, cross; *aill*, hill.

CROWNS HILL. Round hill. *Cruinn*, round. S represents inn wrongly supposed to be a plural termination.

CUFFABOUTS. Fold at a small house. *Cuith*, fold; *a'*, of the; *buthan*, small house. Th became ff, and an of *buthan* was improperly made s.

CULTRIG. Burn of the hill slope. *Coill*, hill burn; *ruigh*, slope. T had been added to *coill*, and h had been dropped from *ruigh*.

CULTRIG BENT. Cultrig hill. *Beinn*, hill. T had been added for euphony. See Cultrig.

CULTSYKEFOOT. Hill burn fold. Cult for *coilltean*, little hill; syke, small burn; *chuit, cuit* aspirated, fold. Ch had become ph, equal to f.

CUNINGAR. Rabbit warren. *Coinniceir* (Irish), rabbit warren.

CUTHILL. Fold. *Cuthail*, fold.

DAINTYDODS. Stronghold on a knoll. *Daingneach*, fort, fortified fold; *cnocan*, little hill. An had improperly been made p

DALES. Little meadow. *Dailean*, small riverside field Ean was wrongly changed to s

DALMENY Field of smallness, or small field. *Dail*, field , *mine*, smallness, small The reference must be to the site of the ancient church.

DEACON'S STONE. Stone of parting drinks *Clach* (translated), stone , *deochan*, drinks. An had normally become s, but it should not have been added to an

DEAN. Den. *Dein*, den, valley eroded by ice or by running water.

DEANFORTH COTTAGE Cottage at a fold in a den. *Dein*, dean, den, ravine ; *chorth*, *corth* aspirated, fold. Ch became ph, equal to f.

DEANS. Little den. *Deinan*, diminutive of *dein*, den. An had improperly been changed to s.

DECHMONT. Good hill *Deagh*, good, beautiful ; *monadh*, hill.

DECHMONT LAW Hill of Dechmont. *Lamh*, hill. Mh is equivalent to w.

DEIL'S KITCHEN Cattlefold. *Cuithan*, diminutive of *cuith*, fold. Th had been strengthened by the insertion of c Deil's, for devil's, is sometimes prefixed to a work which seems to be greater than human power could have produced or than human want required.

DOGHILLOCK, for *Dubh Chnocan*. Black hillock. *Dubh*, black , *chnocan*, *cnocan* aspirated, hillock. Bh had become gh, and subsequently h had been lost, and latterly *chnocan* had been translated into hillock

DOLPHINGTON. Black hill town. *Doille*, darkness, dark ; *fin*, hill.

DOOMSDALE. Field near a hill. *Dun*, hill , *dail*, field. N had become m, and s had been inserted because *dun* had been supposed to be plural.

DOVEHILL Black hill. *Dubh*, black

DRUID'S TEMPLE. Stone circle round a grave. In the reign of Charles II., John Aubrey, an English antiquary, said the stone circles were Druidical places of worship.

DRUM Long hill. *Druim*, ridge like the back of a beast.

DRUM SANDS. Ridge of sand. *Druim*, long back, ridge.

DRUMBEG Small ridge. *Druim*, ridge , *beag*, small.

DRUMBOWIE Yellow hill *Druim*, ridge ; *buidhe*, yellow

DRUMCROST. Cross over a long hill. *Crois*, crossing ; *druim*, ridge.

DRUMDUFF. Black hill. *Druim*, ridge , *dubh*, black.

DRUMELZIE, for *Druimmellan*. Both parts mean hill. *Druim*, ridge, long hill ; *mellan*, small round hill.

DRUMFORTH. Hill of the fold. *Druim*, ridge, long hill ; *chorth*, *corth* aspirated, fold. Ch had become ph, which is f.

DRUMLYON. Hill of the level plain. *Druim*, ridge; *lean*, level ground.

DRUMSHORELAND. Drumshore represents *Druim Sear*. Dark ridge. *Druim*, ridge; *sear*, dark. *Sear* is pronounced shar. Land is *lamhan*, hill, with mh silent and euphonic d added to an. *Lamhan* had been added to explain the preceding part.

DRUMTASSIE. Warm hill. *Druim*, hill, long ridge; *teasach*, warm.

DUBHALL, for *Dubh Choill*. Black hill. *Dubh*, black; *choill*, *coill* aspirated, hill. C in ch had been lost, being silent.

DUBS. Little black place. *Dubhan*, diminutive of *dubh*, black. An had wrongly been made s.

DUDDINGSTON, for *Baile Dubh Dun*. Town on a black hill. *Baile*, town; *dubh*, black; *dun*, hill.

DUMBACK, for *Dun Bac*. Hill of the moss. *Dun*, hill; *bac*, peat moss.

DUNCANSEAT. Site of a fold. Seat is *suidhe*, place, site. *Duncan* had originally been *chuitail*, *cuitail* aspirated, fold, which had been corrupted into whitehill. This had been turned into Gaelic by *duncan*, white hill (*dun*, hill; *can*, white).

DUNDAS. Hill of the burn. *Dun*, hill; with euphonic d added; *eas* (pronounced as), burn, water.

DUNTARVIE, for *Dun Tearbhadh*. Hill of division. *Dun*, hill; *tearbhadh*, for *tearbadh*, division. Bh is equal to v.

DUNTER HILL. *Dun Tir*. Hill land. *Dun*, hill; *tir*, land.

DURHAMSTOWN. Town on a stream. *Dobhar* (bh silent), water; *amhainn*, river. Ainn became s, abnormally.

DYE WATER. Black burn. *Dubh*, black.

DYKE. *Dubh*, black. Bh had become ch, and h had been lost.

DYKEHEAD. Black fold. *Dubh*, black; *chuid*, *cuid* aspirated, fold. C had been lost, and huid became head.

DYKENOOK. Turn in the line of an embankment. Dyke, wall in Scotland, but ditch in England; nook, angle, corner.

DYLAND. Black hill. *Dubh*, black; *lamhan*, hill. Mh silent had been omitted and euphonic d had been added to n.

EAGLE ROCK. Rock at a fold. *Chuitail*, *cuitail* aspirated, fold, corrupted into whitehill, which was again turned into Gaelic by *aodgeal*, white hill (*aod*, brae, hill; *geal*, white). *Aodgeal* has now become eagle.

EASTON. Town at a stream. *Eas*, burn, stream. *Eas* is pronounced like ace, sometimes as ess, and in England it is usually made ash at the beginning of a name.

ECCLESMACHAN. Fold in a small plain. *Chuitail*, *cuitail* aspirated, fold; *maghan*, small plain. *Chuitail* became white-hill, which was made in Gaelic *aoageal*, white hill (*aod*, hill, brae; *geal*, white). In *aodgeal* o is silent and was lost, and by suppression of d it became ageal, which became eccle, aigle, eagle, etc.

ECHLINE Place at a pool. *Achadh*, place ; *linne*, pool. Dh in *achadh* is silent, and it and its vowel had been lost.

EEL ARK. Place where eels accumulated in their progress to the sea in autumn. Ael (Anglo-Saxon), eel ; airc, ark, receptacle.

ELDBICK, for *Ruigh Aill*. Slope of the hill. *Ruigh*, slope ; *aill*, hill.

ENTRYFOOT. Hill of the fold. *An*, the ; *triath*, hill ; *chuit*, *cuit* aspirated, fold. Ath silent had been lost, and ch had become ph, equal to f.

ERRICK BURN. Burn of the shieling on the slope of a hill. *Airidh*, shieling ; *ruigh*, slope of a hill.

FAIRNIEHILL Hill where alders grow. *Fearnach*, abounding in alders.

FAIRY LEAP. Turn of the hill. *Luib*, bend, turn ; *faire*, hill.

FALLSIDE. Site of a fold. *Suidhe*, site ; *fal*, fold

FAULDHOUSE. Both parts mean fold Fauld sometimes means a small enclosed arable field, and sometimes the fold in which cattle were penned at night. House is *chuith*, *cuith* aspirated, fold. C was lost, th became sh, and h was lost leaving huis, now become house. The second part may be the older.

FAWNSPARK. Enclosed place with a gentle slope. *Pairc*, park ; *fan*, gentle slope. S represents an in *fan*, which had wrongly been regarded as a plural termination.

FIVESTANKS, for *Sithean Chuith*. Hill of the fold. *Sithean*, hill , *chuith*, *cuith* aspirated, fold. *Sithean* became stanks by loss of i and h, insertion of euphonic k, and addition of s because *sithean* ended in ean, erroneously regarded as a plural termination Ch of *chuith* became ph or f, and th became bh or v.

FOLLY BRIDGE. Bridge on the way to a hill. *Choille*, *coille* aspirated, hill. Ch had become ph equal to f.

FORKNEUK. Corner suitable for growing oats. *Chorc*, *corc* aspirated, oats. Ch had become ph, equal to f, and c had been changed to k.

FOULDUBS. Black pool. *Pollan*, diminutive of *poll* ; *dubh*, black. S represents an of *pollan* regarded as a plural termination.

FOULSHIELS, for *Pholl Sealan*. Pool on a shieling. *Pholl*, *poll* aspirated, pool, burn ; *sealan*, shieling, pasture among hills. Shiels is a mistake for shieling. *Sealan*, is both the plural of *seal*, shiel, and the singular of *sealan*, a shieling.

FOXHALL. Fox hill. Hall is *choill*, *coill* aspirated, hill, with c silent lost, and oi changed to a.

GALA BRAES. Cattlefold. Originally *chuitail*, *cuitail* aspirated, fold. *Chuitail* was corrupted into whitehill, which was afterwards turned into Gaelic by *gealach braighean*, white hill (*gealach*, white ; *braighean*, diminutive of *braigh*, hill).

GALESHIELS, for *Sealan Chuit*, Shiels at a fold. *Sealan*, shiels, huts on summer pasture ; *chuit*, *cuit* aspirated, fold. Se in *sealan* is equal to she, and an normally became s. *Chuit* was corrupted into white, which was made in Gaelic *gealach*, white, now gale.

GALLOWS KNOWE. Knoll where criminals were hanged on a gallows, after being convicted at a burgh court.

GALLOWSCROOK. Gallows hill. Crook is for *cnoc*, hill.

GARDENERS HILL, GARDNERS HALL. Rough hill of the shieling. *Garbh*, rough; *dun*, hill; *airidh*, shieling. S was inserted to make gardener and gardner possessive. Hall is for *choill, coill* aspirated, hill. C silent had been lost, and oi had become a. *Choill* had been added to explain *dun*.

GATEHOUSE. Windy fold. *Gaothach*, windy; *chuith, cuith* aspirated, fold. *Chuith* lost c, and th became sh, which afterwards lost h. Huis became house.

GATESIDE. Windy place. *Gaothach*, windy; *suidhe*, place.

GILL BURN. Burn of the fold. Gill had originally been *chuith, cuith* aspirated, fold, which had been corrupted into white, and this had afterwards been turned into Gaelic by *geal*, white, now made gill.

GLADEHILL. Kite hill. Glede (English), kite.

GLENBARE. Glen of the path. *Gleann*, glen; *bair*, beaten path, road.

GLENDAVON. Glen of the two streams. *Gleann*, glen; *da*, two; *abhainn*, stream.

GLENMAVIS, for *Gleann Maitheas*. Glen of goodness. *Gleann*, glen; *maitheas*, goodness. Th became bh, equal to v.

GLENPUNTIE. Glen of the fold. *Gleann*, glen; *pundan*, diminutive of *pund*, fold, pound for straying cattle. An became ie normally.

GLENPUTTIE, for *Gleann Chuitan*. Glen of the little fold. *Gleann*, glen; *chuitan, cuitan* aspirated, small fold. Ch had become ph, which became p by loss of h. An normally became ie.

GORMYRE. Green myre. *Gorm*, green.

GOWAN BANK. Fold. *Gabhann* fold. Bank had originally been *chuit, cuit* aspirated, fold, which was corrupted into white. This was afterwards made in Gaelic *ban*, white, to which was added euphonic k. Bh in *gabhann* is equal to w.

GOWAN BRAE. Brae growing gowans. *Gabhann*, fold, daisy —because its petals are arranged like the trunks of trees enclosing folds.

GOWAN STANK. Ditch near a fold. *Gabhann*, fold; *stagnum* (Latin), standing water, slow-running, deep ditch. Bh is equal to w.

GRAHAMSDYKE. Dyke constructed for warlike purposes. *Grimeasach*, surly, rugged, martial. Dyke probably means the great ditch on the north side of the Roman wall. In England dyke usually means ditch.

GRANGE. Farm belonging to a religious convent. Granum (Latin), grain.

GRANGEPANS. Pans at Grange where salt water was boiled dry in making salt. *Panna*, pan.

GREENDYKES. This name implies that the wall of the fold at the place had been constructed of earth, which was green on the outside

GREENRIG. Green slope. *Ruigh*, slope of a hill.

GREIG'S HILL The second part is a translation of the first *Creag*, hill

GROUGHFOOT. Fold *Crubh*, fold; *chuit*, fold. Bh had become gh, ch had become ph or f, and crughfuit had lapsed into groughfoot.

HADDIE'S WALLS, for *Bhailean Aodann*. Small town on a brae. *Bhailean, bailean* aspirated, small town, *aodann*, brae. Bh became w, and ean became s instead of ie H was prefixed to *aodann*, and ann became both ie and s.

HAGS BRAE. Hill of moss-pots. *Braigh*, hill, hag (Scotch), hole out of which peats had been dug.

HAINNINGS. Small fold *Fhaingan, faingan* aspirated, small fank or sheepfold. F, being silent, had been lost, g had also been lost, and an had been made ing but it had also been regarded as a plural termination and made s. *Faingan* is formed from *faing*, the genitive of *fang*, fank.

HALFLAND SYKE. Halfland is for *Chabh Lamhan* Hollow of the little hill. *Chabh, cabh* aspirated, hollow, *lamhan*, diminutive of *lamh*, hill C of *chabh* had been lost, being silent, l had been inserted though not sounded; bh had become ph or f; mh had been lost, being silent, and euphonic d had been added to an. Syke is a very small stream

HALL BATHGATE. Hill of Bathgate *Choill, coill* aspirated, hill C, being silent, was lost, and oi became a to produce an English word.

HANGINGSIDE, for *Suidhe Fhangan* Place of the small fank. *Suidhe*, place; *fhangan, fangan* aspirated, small fold or fank. F had been lost, and g had been inserted to obtain an English word with a meaning.

HARDHILL The second part is a translation of the first. *Ard*, hill Euphonic h had been prefixed to *ard*.

HAREMOSS. Moss of the shieling. *Airidh*, shieling Euphonic h had been prefixed, and idh had become silent and had been lost Moss may represent *mosaiche*, dirty wet place. The last part of *mosaiche* would readily be lost.

HAWK HILL. Hill frequented by hawks in search of mice, beetles, etc. Hawk is sometimes a corruption of *achadh*, place.

HAWTHORNSYKE, for *Choill Charn* Syke. Small burn draining a hill. *Choill, coill* aspirated, hill, *charn, carn* aspirated, hill; syke, from *sugh*, wet place, head of a burn *Choill* had lost initial c and had become hall, which had been corrupted into ha', afterwards made haw. The name Hawthornsyke Burn is not appropriate for the burn passing Binn's Mill.

HAY HILL. Hill of the fold. *Chuith, cuith* aspirated, fold.

C and th, being silent, had been lost.   Hui had been pronounced as hey, which became hay.

HAYSCRAIGS, for *Creagan Chuithan*.   Rocks at a little fold. *Creagan*, plural of *creag*, rock; *chuithan, cuithan* aspirated, little fold.   C of ch had been lost, th had also been lost, and an had abnormally been made s.

HEADS.   Little fold.   *Chuidan, cuidan* aspirated, diminutive of *cuid*, fold.   C in ch had been lost, and an was wrongly made s instead of ie.   Huids became heads.

HEIGHTS.   Small fold.   *Chuidhan, cuidhan* aspirated, small fold.   C had been lost; dh had become gh, with euphonic t added; and an became s.

HERMIT'S HOUSE   House occupied by a hermit.   Eremites (Greek), desert-dweller.

HIDDLEFAULDS.   Small enclosed fields at a cattlefold. *Chuidail*, fold.   C silent had been lost.

HILDERSTON.   Town at a small hill   *Choill, coill* aspirated, hill; *der* (Irish), small.   S was added to obtain a possessive.

HILLHOUSE   Hill of the fold.   *Chuith, cuith* aspirated, fold. C was lost, and th became sh, from which h was afterwards lost, leaving huis, now made house.

HILTLY for *Allt Lamh*.   Burn of the hill.   *Allt*, burn; *lamh* (mh silent), hill.   Euphonic h had been prefixed to *allt*.

HOLEHOUSEBURN.   Burn of the hill of the fold.   *Choill, coill* aspirated, hill; *chuith, cuith* aspirated, fold.   C in ch is silent, th became sh and s by loss of h.   Huis became house.

HOLMES.   Low land near a river.   Holm (English), low ground.   S is sometimes added to names of places to make them possessives.

HOLYGATE, for *Gaothach Choille*.   Windy hill.   *Gaothach*, windy; *choille, coille* aspirated, hill.   C had been aspirated because the adjective preceded the noun, but c becoming silent had been lost.

HOPEFIELD.   Field of the hill; *chop, cop* aspirated, hill.   C had been lost, being silent.

HOPETOUN.   Hill town.   *Chop, cop* aspirated, hill.   C, being silent, had been lost; and e had been added to obtain a name with a meaning, however inappropriate.

HOUND POINT.   Projecting point of a hill.   *Fhin, fin* aspirated, hill.   F in fh is usually lost, and d is often added to n. In several names in Aberdeenshire i in *fin* becomes u, as in Ord Fundlie.

HOUSTON, for *Baile Chobhan*   Town in the hollow.   *Baile*, town; *chobhan, cobhan* aspirated, hollow.   C in ch had been lost, being silent, bh had become ou, and an had wrongly been regarded as a plural termination and had been changed to s.

HUMBIE.   Small hill.   *Thoman, toman* aspirated, little hill.

T silent had been lost, euphonic b had been added to m, and an had become ie.

HUNTBURN. Burn where assemblies were held. *Choinne, coinne* aspirated, meeting. C silent had been lost.

HUNTER'S CRAIG. Rock at which meetings were held. *Creag,* rock ; *choinne, coinne* aspirated, meeting.

ILLIESTON. Place in a nook. *Uileann,* nook. Eann had become ie.

INCH, for *Innis* Enclosed place, fold.

INCH GARVIE. Rough island *Innis,* island ; *garbhach,* rough

INCHCROSS Enclosed place at a cross. *Innis,* enclosure ; *crois,* cross.

INKS. Fold Originally *Chuitail, cuitail* aspirated, fold, corrupted into whitehill, which was made in Gaelic *fhincan,* white hill (*fhin, fin* aspirated, hill ; *can,* white). Fh had been lost, and an became s, improperly. Incs is now inks.

INVERAVON. Infall of the Avon. *Inbhir,* infall ; *abhainn,* river

JACK'S HOUSES, for *Chuithan Iochd* Small fold in a hollow. *Chuithan, cuithan* aspirated, small fold , *iochd,* howe C silent had been lost, th had become sh, and afterwards h had been lost. An had improperly become s. *Iochd* became Jock, and Jock became Jack.

JINKABOUT MILL, for *Dun a' Buth* Mill. Knoll of the hut mill. *Dun,* knoll, with euphonic k added , *a',* of the , *buth,* house, hut. The knoll is at Inveravon.

JOCKS HILL, JOCK'S HOLE. Hill in a hollow. *Iochd,* hollow, *choill, coill* aspirated, hill. Hole is the same as hill.

KELMANHEAD, for *Chuid Caol Man* Fold in a narrow place on a hill *Chuid, cuid* aspirated, fold , *caol,* narrow hollow ; *man,* hill. *Chuid* had been aspirated when it was put last and then c had been dropped.

KEPSKAITH. Plot of ground at the burn of the fold. *Ceap,* plot , *eas,* burn ; *cuith,* fold. There is a plot of ground between two burns, which might have been the fold Ea of *eas* coalesced with s and was lost. *Eas* sounds ace, ess, and ash.

KETTLESTON. Town at a fold. *Cuitail,* fold. S makes kettle possessive.

KILPUNT. Head of the pound Cill for *ceann,* head , *pund,* pound for straying cattle.

KINGLASS, for *Ceann Leas.* Head of the fold. *Ceann,* head , *leas,* a variant of *lios,* fold.

KINGS. Little head *Ceann,* head. *Ceann* became cinn, to which s had been added because eann was supposed to be a plural termination. G had been added to obtain an English word.

KINGSCAVIL. King's share. *Cabhuil,* net, basket, lot.

KINGSFIELD. Head of the field *Ceann,* head , *achadh,* field *Ceann* had been corrupted into king, to which s had been added because eann had wrongly been thought to be a plural termination

KINNEIL. Head of the hill. *Ceann*, head ; *aill*, hill.

KINNEN HILL. Small hill. *Ceannan*, diminutive of *ceann*, head.

KIPPS. Small hill. *Ceapan*, small hill. S represents an, erroneously regarded as a plural termination.

KIRKLAND. Both parts mean hill. *Creag*, hill ; *lamhan*, hill. Mh is silent and had been lost. D had been added to an for euphony.

KIRKLISTON. Church at the town of the fold. *Lios*, fold.

KIRKROADS, for *Ruighean Creag*. Little slope of the hill. *Ruighean*, diminutive of *ruigh*, slope, shieling ; *creag*, hill. An had been regarded as a plural termination and had been made s instead of ie. Gh and dh are interchangeable, both being equal to y.

KIRKTON. Hill town. *Creag*, hill.

KNAPPERS. Head of the little shieling. *Cnap*, knoll ; *airidhean*, diminutive of *airidh*, shieling. Idh was lost, being silent, and ean became s instead of ie.

KNIGHTSRIDGE. Slope of a hill. *Ruigh*, slope ; *cnoc*, hill. In Gaelic the term for a knight is *cniochd*, which has some resemblance to *cnoc*, hill.

KNOCK. Hill. *Cnoc*, hill.

KNOWS. Knoll. *Cnocan*, diminutive of *cnoc*, hill An should have become ie, being a diminutive termination.

LAIGHLANDS, for *Fhliuch Lamhan*. Wet little hill. *Fhliuch*, *fliuch* aspirated, wet ; *lamhan*, diminutive of *lamh*, hill. Th is silent and had been dropped, ch had become gh, mh being silent had been lost, and the diminutive termination had wrongly been made s, and instead of being substituted for an it had been added to it. D had been inserted after an for euphony.

LAMPINSDUB, for *Lamhan Dubh*. Black little hill. *Lamhan*, little hill ; *dubh*, black. S represents an of *lamhan*, erroneously thought to be a plural termination. Mh of *lamhan* had been confused with ph.

LANGSIDE, for *Suidhe Lamhan*. Place on a hill. *Suidhe*, place ; *lamhan*, hill. Mh, equal to nasal v, was lost but through its influence final n became ng.

LATCH BURN. Burn from a wet place. *Latach*, mire, wet place. By loss of a in ach c was softened, and ch is pronounced as in English words.

LAW. Hill. *Lamh*, hill.

LAWFLAT. Court hill. *Lamh*, hill ; *flatha* (Irish), court, session.

LEARIELAW. Hill with a sloping green side. *Lamh*, hill ; *leargan*, slope, green side. Gh is equal to y and y would have coalesced with ie.

LEUCHOLD. Wet burn. *Fhliuch*, wet, marshy ; *allt*, burn. Fh is usually silent and had been lost.

LIGGATE SKYE. Syke of the milking fold. *Leigeadh*, milking.

LINDSAY'S CRAIGS, for *Creagan Lean Saimh.* Little hill of the quiet plain. *Creagan,* diminutive of *creag,* hill; *lean,* plain; *saimh,* tranquillity, quietness. S makes Lindsay possessive.

LINKS Level grassy terraces near the sea. *Lianan,* plural of *lian,* level place. Euphonic c had been added to *lian,* and an had become s. Liancs has now become links. Places called links are usually ancient beaches raised to 25 and 50 feet above sea level

LINLITHGOW, for *Linne Lios Cuith.* Pool of the enclosure at the fold. *Linne,* pool, lake; *lios,* enclosure; *cuith,* fold Final th is silent.

LINN-MILL. Mill at a waterfall *Linne,* pool, waterfall

LIVINGSTON. Beautiful town. *Liomhanach,* bright, beautiful. Mh is equal to v. Ach had been lost, ch being silent.

LOANHEAD. Head of a grassy place. *Lean,* level grassy place.

LOANINGHILL. Hill of the little grassy place *Leanan,* diminutive of *lean,* grassy place.

LOCHCOTE. Fold at a loch. *Cuit,* fold.

LOGIE VALE. Little howe valley. *Lagan,* diminutive of *lag,* howe

LONG LIVINGSTON. Hill of Livingston. *Lamhan,* hill. Mh is equal to nasal v and though mh had been lost by its influence n became ng, and *lamhan* became lang, subsequently anglicised into long.

LONGCROFT. Hill croft. *Lamhan,* diminutive of *lamh,* hill. Mh had been lost, and la-an had become lang because mh is nasal, and then lang had become long.

LONGRIDGE. Slope of the hill. *Lamhan,* hill; *ruigh,* slope of a hill. *Lamhan* became lang by loss of mh and the addition of g to an. Lang was anglicised into long

LOOKABOUTYE This name may be English as the place is in an elevated situation. It may, however, be a slightly different version of an Aberdeenshire name Titaboutie, which probably represents *Taiteach Buthan,* pleasant house, in which an has become ie.

MACKIE'S KNOWES. Knoll in a plain. *Cnocan,* diminutive of *cnoc,* hill , *maghan,* diminutive of *magh,* plain. An of cnocan was made es instead of ie, and an of *maghan* becomes ies, some regarding it as a diminutive and others as a plural termination.

MAD BURN. Burn of the plain. *Magh,* plain.

MAGGIE'S WELL Well in a little howe *Maghan,* diminutive of *maghan,* little howe. An became ie normally.

MAILING BURN. Burn from a little hill. *Meallan,* diminutive of *meall,* hill.

MAINS BURN. Burn of the hill. *Man,* hill. S represents an of *man,* erroneously regarded as a plural termination.

MALLENS BURN. Burn of the little hill. *Meallan,* diminutive of *meall,* hill. An had improperly been made s and added to *meallan.*

c

MANNERSTON, for *Baile Man Airidh.* Town on the hill of the shieling. *Baile,* town; *man,* hill; *airidh,* shieling. S is an insertion made to obtain a possessive. Idh in airidh is usually silent.

MANSGROVE. Grove on a hill *Man,* hill. S represents an regarded as a plural termination, which it is not.

MARY BAILLIE'S WELL, for *Tobar Baile Murean.* Well at a town on a small hill. *Tobar,* well; *baile,* town; *murean,* small hill. Ean normally became y.

MERRYLEES. Little hill with a fold on it. *Murean,* little hill; *lios,* fold. Ean normally became y.

MIDDLERIG. Middle of the slope on a hillside. *Ruigh,* slope on a hill.

MIDHOPE. Middle hill. *Chop,* cop aspirated, hill. C in ch is silent and had been omitted.

MILKHOUSES. Houses where cows on summer pastures had been milked.

MILLCRAIG. Both parts mean hill. *Mill,* second form of *meall,* hill; *creag,* hill.

MILLRIG. Slope of the hill. *Ruigh,* lower slope of a hill; *mill,* second form of *meall,* hill.

MINGLE PIT. Place at a fold. Mingle had originally been *Chuitail,* cuitail aspirated, fold, corrupted into whitehill. This had been turned into Gaelic by *moinegeal,* white hill (*moine,* moor, hill; *geal,* white).

MOAT KNOWE. Knoll at which barony courts were held. *Mod,* court of justice.

MOCHRIE'S HILL. Dark slope of a hill. *Muich,* dark; *ruighean,* diminutive of *ruigh,* slope. Ch is equal to y and had been lost. Ean was properly made ie, but it was also improperly made s, and both were put to the end of the name. The colour of a hill told whether it afforded good pasture or not.

MONS HILL. Hill. *Man,* hill. S had been added because an is sometimes a plural termination.

MOSSHALL. Farm house in a moss. Hall, public place in a house.

MOSSHOUSE. Fold in a moss. *Chuith,* cuith aspirated, fold; *mosaiche,* moss, filthy place. C in ch had been lost, and th had become sh, afterwards losing h.

MOUNT MICHAEL. Black hill mount. *Muiche,* blackness, black, dark; *aill,* hill.

MOUNTHOOLY. Both parts of the name mean hill. *Monadh,* hill; *choille, coille* aspirated, hill. C silent had been lost.

MOUNTJOY. Black mount. *Dubh,* black; *monadh,* hill. D in Gaelic frequently becomes j in English.

MUCKRAW. Swinefold. *Muc,* pig; *rath* (th silent), fold.

MUIREND. Small hill. *Murean,* diminutive of mur, hill.

MUIRHALL Farm house on a muir.

MUIRHOUSE. Fold on a moor. House had been in Gaelic *chuith, cuith* aspirated, fold. C had been lost, being silent, and th had become sh, which afterwards lost h. Then huis had become house

MUIRHOUSES. Houses on a moor.

MUIRIEHALL. Both parts of the name mean hill. *Murean,* diminutive of *mur,* hill; *choill, coill* aspirated, hall. Ean had normally become ie, and oi had become a.

MURRAYFIELD Field of the hill burn *Mur,* hill; *abh,* burn, water.

MURRAYGATE, for *Cuit Mur Abh.* Fold at the hill burn. *Cuit,* fold, *mur,* hill; *abh,* burn. C of *cuit* had become first ch and then gh, which had lost h. Bh had become gh which is equal to y.

MYRE. In Scotch, myre usually means a bog from which a small stream is discharged.

NANCY'S HILL. The hill *An,* the; *sith* (th silent), hill Euphonic n had been prefixed to an, and s had been added to make Nancy possessive

NETHERHOUSES. Lower little fold Houses is for *Chuithan, cuithan* aspirated, little fold C had been lost; th had become sh, from which h had been lost, and an had improperly been changed into es. Huises has become houses.

NETTLEHILL. Nettle is for *Net Lamh.* Burn of the hill. *Net,* burn, *lamh* (mh silent), hill Hill is a translation of *lamh.*

NEW ENGLAND. New in names may represent three things. (1) The English word new. (2) *Naomh* (pronounced nuv or new), sacred, belonging to a church or a convent. (3) *An Chuith,* the fold, with the aspirated letters dropped. The remainder ui has become ewe in several names, and an and ui combined would sound anew, from which a would be dropped

England represents *An Lamhan.* The little hill. *An,* the; *lamhan* (mh silent), little hill For euphony g was added to *an* and d to *lamhan.* New England probably means the fold on the little hill.

NEW GARDENS, for *An Chuith Garbh Dunan.* The fold on the rough little hill. *An,* the; *chuith, cuith* aspirated, fold; *garbh,* rough, *dunan,* little hill, with an improperly changed to s. See New England.

NEW MAINS. New farm instead of a former, occupied by the proprietor of an estate. Terrae Dominicales (Latin), lord's lands through French demesnes, in English made domains See New England

NEWHALLS, for *Naomh Choillean.* Sacred little hill. *Naomh,* belonging to a church or a convent, sacred; *choillean, coillean* aspirated, little hill C silent had been lost, and ean had improperly been made s instead of ie. Oi and a are sometimes interchanged. See New England.

NEWLISTON. New town at a fold. *Lios,* fold. See New England.

NEWYEARFIELD. Field of the fold on a shieling. *Achadh,* field, place; *an,* of the; *chuith, cuith* aspirated, fold; *airidh,* shieling. *An* lost a, *chuith* lost its aspirated letters, and *airidh* lost dh and its vowel.

NIDDRY. Slope at a burn. *Ruigh,* slope; *nid,* burn.

OATRIDGE, for *Ruigh Chuit.* Slope of the fold. *Ruigh,* slope; *chuit, cuit* aspirated, fold. Ch had become silent and had been lost. Then uit became oat.

OCHILTREE. Small hill. *Ogail,* small; *triath* (th silent), hill.

PADDOCKHALL. Farm house at a small hump. *Pait,* hump; *og,* little; hall, farm house with a large kitchen, the public part of the house.

PALACE WOOD. Wood at a protected fold. *Peall,* protection by a wall, skins or mats; *lios,* fold.

PAN BRAES. Braes where salt water was evaporated in making salt. *Panna* (Irish), pan.

PARDOVAN, for *Cnap Airidh Dubh Abhainn.* Knoll of the shieling at the black burn. *Cnap,* knoll, top; *airidh,* shieling; *dubh,* black; *abhainn,* stream. Cna of *cnap* had been lost perhaps after c had been aspirated. Bh is equal to v, but the second bh had been lost.

PARK. Enclosed field. *Pairc,* park. Before 1750 so few fields were enclosed that park was a distinctive name.

PARKLY CRAIGS, for *Pairc Lamh,* and *Creagan* added to explain *Lamh.* Park hill. *Pairc,* park; *lamh* (mh silent), hill; *creagan,* diminutive of *creag,* hill. An should have been made ie, not s.

PEACE HILL, PEACE KNOWE. Small hill, and Small knowe. *Pios,* small.

PEATDRAUGHT BAY. The meaning of the name is obscure. Peatdraught might represent *Pait Draigh,* hump growing thorntrees. *Pait,* hump; *draigh,* thorntree. Bay might represent *bathaiche,* cow-house, contracted to bai by loss of the aspirated letters.

PEEL. Protected place. *Peall,* skin, wall, protection against thieves or against inclement weather.

PEPPER HILL. Hill of the fold on the shieling. *Cuith,* fold; *airidh,* shieling. Ch and th had both become ph and afterwards h in both had been lost. This left puip, which when sounded with a small round opening between the lips became peep.

PETERSHILL. Hill of the hump. *Pait,* hump. Peter and Patrick and their familiar diminutives Pete, Pettie, and Pattie, are confounded with one another, and *pait,* hump, had been thought to be connected with Peter. S turned Peter into a possessive.

PHILPSTOUN, PHILPSTON. Farm town on a small hill. *Coillean,* small hill, which had lapsed into *cuilean,* little dog. This had been turned into whelp in English and folp in Scotch, which became Philp in some names and Philip in others. Another Philip comes from a Greek word meaning lover of horses.

PILGRIM'S HILL. If this name is of Gaelic origin it means protected place or fold on a barren hill. *Peall*, peel, protected place, fold ; *grimeasach*, barren, rugged

POLKEMMET. Crooked burn *Pall*, burn, pool , *Caimead*, crookedness, crooked.

POORWIFE'S BRAE. Brae of the little fold. Poor has the meaning small Wife's represents *chuithan*, *cuithan* aspirated, fold Ch may become bh, equal to w, and th may become ph, equal to f. An should normally have become ie, but having been thought to be a plural termination it had become es. *Chuithan* has become wife's in an Aberdeenshire name

PORT BUCHAN Port on the Union Canal at a curve. *Port*, harbour , *bogha*, little curve, bend.

PORT EDGAR. Harbour at a rough brae. *Aod*, brae , *garbh* (bh silent), rough.

PORTERSIDE. Meaning uncertain Perhaps site of the entrance to the shieling. *Suidhe*, site ; *port*, gate, entrance ; *airidh*, shieling

POTTISHAW. Wood at a small pot in a burn. *Poitean*, small pot. Ean normally became i (for ie).

POWFLATS. Flat places near a burn. *Poll*, burn.

PRESTON. Town at a bushy place. *Preas*, bush.

PRIEST MILL. Mill at a bushy place. *Preas*, bush, bushy place.

PRIESTINCH Enclosed bushy place *Preas*, bush ; *innis*, enclosed place.

PUNCH WELL. Well at a pound where straying cattle were shut up. *Pund*, pound.

PUNCHEON LAW. Hill of the old pound. *Lamh*, hill , *pund*, pound, pen for straying cattle ; *sean* (pronounced shan), old

PYOTHALL Magpie hall *Piothaid*, magpie.

QUAKER'S QUARRY. Quarry in a cup-shaped hollow. *Cuach*, cup, round hollow.

QUARTER. Enclosed circular place on a shieling *Cuairt*, circle ; *airidh*, shieling.

RASHIERIDGE. Both parts represent *ruigh*, hill slope One part had been added to explain the other

RAVEN CRAIG. Stone circle on a hill. *Rath*, circle round a grave, fold ; *bheinn*, *beinn* aspirated, hill *Creag*, hill, craig, had been added to explain raven.

RED BURN. Burn red with iron oxide.

REDDOCK-HILL. Hill ending in a point *Rudhach*, ending in points.

REEVES, REVESTON. Small slope, and Town on a small slope. *Ruighean*, diminutive of *ruigh*, slope. Ean was improperly made s instead of ie

REVEL BANK. Bank of the slope of the hill. *Ruigh*, slope ; *aill*, hill. Gh had become bh or v.

RICCARTON. Town on the slope of a hill. *Ruigh*, slope , *ard*, hill

RICKLE. Slope of the hill. *Ruigh*, slope ; *aill*, hill The

Rickle is a small island in the loch of Linlithgow. The name would be appropriate for the side of the hill on the north. As a Scotch term rickle means a small rick or pile of stones or peats.

RIGHEAD. Hill of the fold. *Ruigh*, slope, hill; *chuid, cuid* aspirated, fold. C had been lost, being silent.

RIGHOUSE, for *Ruigh Chuith*. Slope of the fold. *Ruigh*, slope; *chuith, cuith* aspirated, fold. *Ruigh* had lost h. *Cuith* lost c silent, and th became first sh and then s by loss of the aspirate h. Huis became house.

RIVALDS GREEN. Green place sloping to a little burn. *Ruigh*, slope; *alltan*, little burn. Gh had become bh, equal to v, and an had become s instead of ie.

ROSE WELL. Well at the point of a field. *Ros*, point.

ROSSHILL, for *Ros Choill*. Point of the hill. *Ros*, point; *choill, coill* aspirated, hill. C silent had been lost, and hoill had become hill. In old Gaelic *coill* means hill, but in modern Gaelic it means wood.

ROSS'S PLANTATION. Ross's represents *ros*, point. The plantation is in a corner between two burns.

ROUGHSYKE. Drain on the slope of a hill. *Ruigh*, slope; syke, beginning of a stream, drain.

ROUND HILL. This is a corruption of *Chruinn Choill*, Round hill. *Chruinn, cruinn* aspirated, round; *choill, coill* aspirated, hill. C of ch in both parts had been lost.

ROUSLAND. Slope of a hill. *Ruigh*, slope at the base of a hill; *lamhan*, diminutive of *lamh*, hill. Euphonic d had been added to n.

RYAL. Hillside. *Ruigh*, slope; *aill*, hill.

SCOTSTON. Town on a burn passing a fold. *Eas* pronounced ess, burn; *cuit*, fold. Ea has been lost because its sound is heard before s.

SEAFIELD. Hill fold. *Sith*, hill.

SHARPSBANK. *Cuit Eas Airidh*. Fold on the burn of the shieling. *Chuit*, fold, corrupted into white, which was turned into Gaelic by *ban*, white, with euphonic k added; *eas* pronounced ash, burn; *airidh*, shieling. *Eas* had lost ea, and dh had become ph, which subsequently lost h.

SLACKEND. Narrow hollow. *Slocan*, diminutive of *sloc*, hollow, gorge.

SNAB. Blunt point. Snub (English), to cut short.

SNIB. Blunt point. Snub, to cut short.

STACKS. Fold made with trunks of trees stuck into the ground. *Stacan*, plural of *stac*, stump of wood.

STANDHILL. The second part is the translation of the first. *Sithean*, hill, corrupted into stan, to which euphonic d had been added.

STANDINGSTONE. Monolith at a pre-Christian grave.

STANEYHILL TOWER, for *Clachach Torr*. Stony hill. *Clachach*, stony; *torr*, steep flat-topped hill, corrupted into tower.

STANKARDS, for *Sithean Ardan*. Little hill. *Sithean*, hill; *ardan*, little hill. *Sithean* became stan, to which euphonic k was added; and an of *ardan* was abnormally changed to s instead of ie.

STARLAW. Hill with a steep bank. *Storr*, steep bank, cliff; *lamh*, hill

STEPEND, STEPENDS. The end of a row of stepping stones across a stream. S probably arose from pronouncing stepend without d and then adding s because en was thought to be a plural termination. Both d and s were added.

STEPPING STONES. A row of stones at intervals for crossing streams and marshy places. In Gaelic a row of stepping stones is *clacharan*, which has often become clatterin or clattering, with bridge added when the stepping stones have given place to a bridge.

STOCK BRIDGE. Bridge formed by a trunk of a tree. *Stoc*, stem, trunk.

STONEHEAD. Stonefold. Head is for *chuid*, *cuid* aspirated, fold C of ch was lost Stone might represent stane, a corruption of *sithean*, hill In this case the name would mean hill of the fold.

STONEHEAP. Both parts mean hill. *Sithean*, corrupted to stane and anglicised to stone, hill , *cheap*, *ceap* aspirated, hill, hillock, hilltop. C in ch had been lost.

STONERIG. Slope of the hill. *Sithean*, hill, *ruigh*, slope. *Sithean* had become stane, which had been anglicised into stone.

STRAND. Small valley. *Srathan*, small valley, with euphonic d added to n. Strachan is another form of *srathan*.

STRATH. Alluvial river valley. *Srath*, flat-bottomed river valley.

STRATHAVON. Valley of the Avon. *Srath*, river valley; *abhainn*, river.

STRATHBROCK. Strath at a hill *Srath*, strath, river valley with alluvial flats ; *bruch*, hill.

STRATHLOANHEAD. Fold in a grassy place in a river valley. *Chuid*, *cuid* aspirated, fold ; *lean*, grassy place, loan ; *srath*, river valley with a flat bottom. *Cuid* had been first, but after aspiration and loss of c it had been put last.

SWINEABBEY. Burn flowing in a marsh. *Sughan* (gh silent), wet ; *abhainn*, stream. Ainn had been regarded as a diminutive termination and had therefore been changed to ey.

SWINEBURN. Burn in a wet marshy place. *Sughan* (gh equal to y), wetness.

SWORDIE. Wet hill. *Sugach*, wet , *ordan*, little hill. An became ie.

SYKE. Drain. *Sugh*, wetness, commencement of a burn in a small eroded valley. Gh had become ch and h had been lost.

TAILEND. Small lump. *Tailean*, diminutive of *tail*, lump.

TANNOCH, for *An t-Aonach*. The hill. *An t*, the , *aonach*, hill.

TANTALLON HILL, for *Tom an t-Allan*. Hill at the burn. *Tom*, hill , *an t*, of the ; *allan*, diminutive of *all*, water.

TAR HILL Steep hill. *Torr*, steep, abrupt hill.

TARRYDEWS. Black little hill. *Torran*, steep round hill *dubh*, black. Bh is equal to w.

TARTRAVEN, for *An t-Ard Rath Bheinn.* The hill of the fold on the hill. *An t*, the; *ard*, height; *rath*, fold; *bheinn, beinn* aspirated, hill. *An t*, kre; *ard* had been prefixed to explain *bheinn*.

TAWNYCRAW. Hill of the fold. *Torr*, steep abrupt hill; *na*, of the; *cra*, wattled fold.

THIRLSTANE. If Scotch this name may have been given to a large stone with a hole in which a gallows-tree was set up. If Gaelic it means stone on a knoll. *Thriath, triath* aspirated, hill, knoll; *aill,* , hill. Ath would have been lost before *aill*.

TIPPET KNOWS, TIPPETHILL. *Taipsach.* Abounding in knolls. In Tippethill the second part is a translation of the first.

TODHOLES. Foxes' holes. Tod (Scotch), fox.

TORBANE. Fold. *Chuitail, cuitail* aspirated, fold. *Chuitail* was corrupted into whitehill, which was made in Gaelic *torrban*, white hill , *torr*, hill; *ban*, white.

TORPHICHEN. Hill of the little fold. *Torr*, hill; *chuithan, cuithan* aspirated, little fold. Ch became ph, and th became ch.

TOTTLY WELLS. Well emitting vapour. *Toitlach*, variant of *toiteach*, giving off vapour. Strong deep-seated springs have water above the temperature of the air in winter, and in calm cold weather vapour rising from them becomes visible like smoke.

TREES. Hill. *Triath*, hill

TRINLYMIRE Mire on a little hill. *Triathan*, diminutive of *triath* (th silent), hill ; *lamh* (mh silent), hill.

TURNHIGH, for *Torran Chuith.* Hill of the fold. *Torran*, small, steep, round hill ; *chuith, cuith* aspirated, fold. C silent was lost, and th became gh, sounded y.

UPHALL, for *A'Choill.* The hill. *A'*, the; *choill, coill* aspirated, hill. Ch became ph, and oi became a.

WALLHOUSE, for *Bhaile Chuith.* Town at a fold. *Bhaile, baile* aspirated, town ; *chuith, cuith* aspirated, fold. Bh is equal to w, and by loss of final e *bhaile* became wall. C in ch had been lost, being silent, and th had become sh, which by loss of h became s. Huis readily lapsed into house.

WALTON. Town on the Roman Wall. The place had been a Roman camp.

WARDLAW. Hill of an enclosure for cattle and sheep. Ward (English), enclosed place ; *lamh*, hill.

WARRENS. Preserves for hares and rabbits.

WATERSTONE, for *Baile Uachdaran.* Town of the chief. *Baile*, town ; *uachdaran*, chief, ruler. Ch had been lost, being silent ; d had been changed to t ; and an having been regarded as a plural termination it had been changed to s.

WELL OF SPA. Well yielding water impregnated with carbonate of iron. The name had been imported from Spa in Belgium, where there are famous chalybeate springs.

WELLHILL Hill of the fold. *Choill, coill* aspirated, hill; *bhuaile, buaile* aspirated, fold. C in ch is silent, and hoill became hill. Bh is equal to w and *bhuaile* became well

WHEATACRE. Fold on hill land. *Chuit, cuit* aspirated, fold; *ard-thir*, high ground (*ard*, height; *thir, tir* aspirated, ground). *Ard-thir* has become acre in the Aberdeenshire name Acrestripe, and Arthur in the Edinburghshire name Arthur's Seat.

WHEATLANDS, for *Lamhan Chuit*. Hill of the fold. *Lamhan* (mh silent), little hill, *chuit, cuit* aspirated, fold. An of *lamhan* had become s, normally; and *chuit*, having lost c, became wheat.

WHINSTONE. Hill stone. *Fhin, fin* aspirated, hill. Th had become wh Whinstone is a hard igneous rock which is usually seen on high ground.

WHITBURN, WHITEBURN. Burn of the fold. *Braon*, burn, *chuit, cuit* aspirated, fold. *Braon* became burn, and *cuit* became whit and white.

WHITDALEHEAD. Fold *Chuidail, cuidail* aspirated, fold, corrupted into whitedale. Head is *chuid, cuid* aspirated, fold, with silent c dropped, added to explain *chuidail* after being corrupted.

WHITE LAW. Fold *Chuitail*, fold, corrupted into whitehill. White remained but hill was translated into Gaelic by *lamh*, hill.

WHITE QUARRIES. Quarries at a fold. White had originally been *chuit, cuit* aspirated, fold, and *chuit* had been corrupted into white.

WHITEBAULKS. Fold in a place where there were ridges of ploughed land. *Chuit, cuit* aspirated, fold, corrupted into white, balks (English), ridges.

WHITEHOUSE. Fold. *Chuit, cuit* aspirated, fold. *Chuit* had been corrupted into white, and to explain it *chuith, cuith* aspirated, fold, had afterwards been added. C in *chuith* had been lost, being silent, and th had become sh. By loss of h huis was left, now become house, but there is no house at Whitehouse.

WHITESIDE. Site of a fold. *Suidhe*, site, *chuit, cuit* aspirated, fold. *Chuit* became white, and *suidhe* became side.

WHITOCK. Small fold. *Chuit, cuit* aspirated, fold; *og*, small.

WILCOXHOLM, WILCOX, for *Uileann Cnocan* Nook of the little hill *Uileann,* corner; cnocan, diminutive of *cnoc*, hill. Eann had become ie, and it had been lost, n in *cnoc* had become silent and had been lost; an had wrongly been made s, which combining with c became x. *Tholm, tolm* aspirated, hill, had been added to *cnocan* as an explanation. T in th is silent and had been lost.

WINCHBURGH, for *Bheinnbruch*. Both parts mean hill. *Bheinn, beinn* aspirated, hill; *bruch*, hill. Bh is equal to w,

D

and *bheinn* had become win, to which c, afterwards made ch, had been added for euphony.

WITCH CRAIG.   Hill of the fold.   *Creag*, hill ; *chuith, cuith* aspirated, fold.   Ch became bh equal to u, v, or w ; and th was strengthened by inserting c between t and h.

WOODCOCKDALE, for *Dail Cnoc Bhad.*   Field of the hill of the wood.   *Dail*, riverside field ; *cnoc*, hill ; *bhad, bad* aspirated, wood.   Bh is equal to w, and wood may be a corruption rather than a translation of *bhad.*

WOOLSTONE, for *Baile Uileann.*   Town in a corner.   *Baile*, town ; *uileann*, nook.   Eann had become ie and had been lost.

WYNDFORD.   Hill ford.   *Bheinn, beinn* aspirated, hill.   Bh is equal to w, and d had been added to nn for euphony.